The Promised Twin

By Kjirstin Youngberg

Published and distributed by:

Granite Publishing and Distribution
270 S Mountainlands Dr.
Orem, UT 84058
(801) 229-9023

ISBN 1-890558-24-9

To Miss Helen Crowell, my guidance counselor at Victor Valley High School. Miss Crowell opened the world to me. She believed in me, and was the first person to teach me I was capable of doing anything I wanted to do; a concept I had never before considered. Thank you, Helen. (It feels good to finally be old enough to call you by your first name.)

ACKNOWLEDGEMENTS

To my husband, Eric, for his constant love and support, and his excellent musical chops. To my family, for their patience through years without a tidy home. To Jill, my strength. To my mother, my anchor. To David, my spirit. To Rachel, my soul. To Jordan, my joy. To Matthew, my heart. To Petrea & Brian K. Kelley for a quarter century of unconditional mentoring. To Julie Dockstader, my alterego. To Liz, Jon, Nicholas & Ariana for their friendship and example. To my editor, John Jones, for his grasp of the obvious, to which I was blind. To my friend, Melinda Hill, a fine writer and constant source of encouragement. To Edna and David Allan and Lorraine and Dr. Philip Washburn, my profound thanks. To my endodontist, Dr. Kent Christiansen, for curing those awful headaches. To my new community and ward, where I truly feel loved, accepted, and at last, home.

The Promised Twin is a book about the life and death of our youngest son, Benjamin Carl Youngberg. It is a personal glimpse into our lives, and our discovery that all life is purposeful and part of a cycle which never ends.

Our Heavenly Father, it is said, knows when every sparrow falls. Through many experiences, I have come to appreciate His will. Life is comfortable when I trust His plan above my own.

While living in France, I received the strongest testimony of not only His constant care, but of our Heavenly Father's precision in putting each person in exactly the right place, and time.

It was 1977, and I was young and foolish. I worked as an *au-pair*, a "Mary Poppins" sort-of nanny for my cousin, Ann, in Biviers, a village in the French Alps. Ann and her husband, Americans with three little girls, were expecting their fourth. (I was hoping they'd get a baby boy, but she had twin girls!) I'd been in Biviers for about three months, and was enjoying a summer Saturday of shopping in Grenoble. Wanting to blend in with the sophisticated, I wore a stylish dress, and very high heels.

Nearly every shop in town had been visited by my feet, and walking on cobblestones had nearly wiped me out.

As I waited at the bus stop, I spotted an athletic shoe store. It would be twenty minutes before my bus would arrive, so I managed to hobble over to buy myself a pair. (I'll never forget the look on the salesman's face. He was aghast that the shoes were for me. When I told him I wanted to wear them home, I thought he'd faint.)

It wasn't my imagination—everyone at the bus stop was openly staring, pointing, and making comments about my running shoes. (This was before running was in vogue, and they were neon blue in a time when everyone in Europe wore subdued hues it; looked strange.

My bus arrived shortly, and I hopped on, but a young man pulled me off. In broken English, he said, "That's not your bus."

Unsure, I re-checked the schedule, and he waved the bus on. It was out of sight by the time I realized that not only was it the right bus, it was the last bus of the day going anywhere near my home.

My temper flared at the young man, who was also a foreigner, and I insisted he call a taxi for me, and that he pay for it. We had a bit of a language problem, and I was furious to find him picking up my packages and walking down the street.

"What are you doing?" I demanded, angrily following him and my packages.

I tried to hail a cab, but realized it would cost a small fortune.

He walked down several streets and alleys I didn't recognize, and I was beginning to understand the seriousness of my predicament.

He stopped at a bar and ordered two drinks. I explained that I didn't drink and wouldn't drink with him if I did. I asked for a telephone and tried to reach my cousin, but there was no answer.

"Nous avons une boisson forte," he said, lightly touching my hand. *"Vous pouvez dormir dans ma maison, et prendre le premier autobus du matin."*

I spoke enough French to understand his suggestion to stay overnight with him and take a bus home in the morning.

He put my packages down to get his drink, and while he was looking the other way I slowly bent down to retrieve them, and backed carefully toward the door.

I ran straight out into the *carrefour*, a busy street intersection, without even looking. I didn't even care if anyone hit me.

The young man was right behind me, and I could hear the other bar patrons laughing and wishing him luck in catching me.

I screamed for help and prayed out loud, and was nearly run over by two young men on bicycles.

Elder's Moyes and Pettengill, Mormon Missionaries, turned their bicycles around and positioned themselves between us.

After a few minutes of flinging French back and forth, the missionaries had me shaking hands with the young man, who returned all my packages and left without a fight.

As we scratched our heads over how to get me home safely, we marveled at the Lord's hand in putting them there for me.

"We're supposed to be in before dark, but we were late tonight," Elder Moyes said.

"Yeah, and we've never gone home this way before," Elder Pettengill added. "We both felt we should turn down this street."

"It's a good thing, too," Elder Moyes said. "He wanted more than a drink with you."

I was still shaking, and looking in awe at my shoes. I couldn't have made ten yards in my heels. I could have been down some dark alley...

Suddenly a big black car pulled alongside us and a man leaned out. In English, he asked if the missionaries were Elder's from The Church of Jesus Christ of Latter-day Saints.

We were stunned. None of us had heard English spoken outside of church for months, and now here it was again!

The man in the car continued, "I'm Fred Stringham from Bountiful, Utah." He introduced his wife and his son, Paul, who had recently been released from his mission. They wanted to know the time and location of church, and they were lost.

We quickly decided if they could drive me home, my cousin could give them directions to *The Three Roses* hotel.

It shouldn't have surprised me, but it did. Once I got them on the right road to get me home, we drove directly past their hotel. It was only a mile from my house.

This experience came back to me as I thought about Ben. I had no doubt that the Lord had a foreknowledge of everything that happened. I couldn't feel sad. Ben's death was part of a larger plan, behind a veil, through which I could not see.

*Matthew on his way to the operating
room—Mt. View Hospital
January 30, 1995*

CHAPTER 1

Move Forward to Reverse

I couldn't breathe. Everything was dark and I was falling; crushed into a sweltering hot tangle of fabric that wrapped itself around me, pulling in every direction. I was suffocating, and I couldn't scream.

"Kjirstin?" a voice called gently through the heat. "Wake up, honey; you're having another bad dream."

My husband, Eric, reached for me in the darkness, softly stroking my shoulder back to reality.

The damp, cotton percale of our sheets clung to my wet skin like melted taffy. Embarrassed, I quietly untangled myself, but a single sob escaped my tightened throat.

"Ben?" Eric asked, trying his best to be understanding.

Though he couldn't see me in the dark, I nodded, and my tears let go like a warm summer rain. My whole body convulsed, and the pain I felt over the death of my baby son would not go away.

"Kjirstin, it was *not* your fault." Eric sighed.

"But it was!" I sobbed. "I *knew* he was going to die. God sent the Holy Ghost to warn me...twice!...but I didn't save him. Don't you think he was sent here because God knew I could save him? He knew I would save him in time. Why didn't I get him? Why?"

Eric had no answers. Perhaps there were no answers. It had been over three years since Benjamin had died, and still I felt no peace.

The next day, I went on with life through my usual routine; phone calls, house cleaning, and decorating for Christmas. It was mid-December, 1994, and we were in our beautiful new home with a view of the snow-covered Sierra Bonita Mountain.

I was preparing dinner when my 12-year-old daughter, Rachel, wandered into the kitchen. She rarely complained about injuries or illness, and I had nearly forgotten that three days before, her finger had been slammed in the gymnasium door at her middle school. She removed the small, plastic bandage and stuck her finger out.

"Look," she said proudly. "It's nearly healed!"

I glanced at her wound and tried not to faint.

"We're going to the doctor," I informed her. "in the car, now."

I gave 14-year-old David instructions on dinner, and asked him to call Dr. Bennett and tell him we were enroute with an infected finger.

Emergency surgery was required. Rachel bit her lip as she tolerated several slow, painful shots of local anesthetic administered directly into her hand and finger. She is one tough kid.

"Stay with me, mom," she pleaded as I tried to slip out the door. "Please don't leave me."

Watching children bleed, is not on top of my "favorite stuff to do" list. I sighed, knowing this was one of those "mother" things, from which there was no escape. I grabbed an office copy of the December 1994 Issue of *Parents Magazine* and tried to focus on that while I held Rachel's other hand.

One article I read held me transfixed. It was in the Our Problem section, and was titled, "Why is our Child so Cranky?" by Jane Marks. It was about Bradley James, a wild little boy with sleep apnea.

Matthew, my three-year-old, was also out of control. So many points in Bradley's story reminded me of Matthew, I was virtually stunned. Matthew snored loudly enough to wake the neighbors. He slept in odd positions. He was cranky and often seemed tired even after a full night's sleep and a nap. Though he was not small for his age when compared to other children, he was much smaller than my other children had been at his age. I attributed this to his being born five weeks prematurely, and because he was a twin.

His twin brother, Benjamin, had died of S.I.D.S. or crib death, in which sleep apnea is often a contributing factor.

I read most of the article aloud, partly to keep Rachel's mind off her finger, but mostly to see if she recognized any of the same problems in Matthew. She did, and added a few of her own I never knew.

"He always wakes up with headaches," she said. "He won't tell you because he hates that liquid medicine you make him swallow."

Dr. Bennett tied the last of Rachel's stitches in a neat, black knot. Her surgery had taken over two hours.

"You're a lucky girl," he said. "You missed infecting that bone by a millimeter or so, but if you'd let that infection go, you could have lost the whole finger. Your nail may grow back—time will tell." Turning to me, he said, "We'll make an appointment for a re-check on Rachel for next week, and if you'd like to bring Matthew in tomorrow, I could take a quick look at his tonsils and adenoids, to see if they're enlarged. He's probably fine, but it never hurts to check."

That night, Matthew crawled into bed with Eric and me as usual at about 1:30 in the morning. His snoring was louder than my husband's by several decibels. I started counting the seconds between his snores. 'Bradley' had held his breath for 22 seconds.

"One-thousand one," I counted, but when Matthew held his breath past thirty seconds, I shook him awake. *"Good grief!"* I thought as reality struck . *"This is serious! I could lose my other baby!"*

Racing downstairs to the basement, I rummaged around for our portable tape recorder. After finding an unused tape, I ran back upstairs and began recording Matthew's snoring.

The next day we saw Dr. Bennett, who referred us to Dr. B. Kelly Ence, an Ear. Nose, and Throat Specialist. After an exam and observation of Matthew, Dr. Ence listened to the tape recording I had made of his snoring. He used a stopwatch to time the intervals between Matthew's breathing. He shook his head and showed me the stopwatch. Forty seconds! My eyes pooled with tears. Matthew had sleep apnea. He'd have to have his tonsils and adenoids removed to prevent damage to his major organs, including his heart.

Surgery was scheduled for Monday, January 30, 1995, at Mountain View Hospital in Payson, Utah. Dr. Ence performed the operation. When it was over, he met me in the waiting room.

"There were some complications," Dr. Ence reported. "but..."

"What happened?" I interrupted. "Can I see him?"

"He's just fine," Dr. Ence continued. "You can go into the recovery room with him now if you like."

Dr. Ence continued to explain what had happened as we walked toward the recovery room, but I was intent upon getting to Matthew, and wasn't really paying much attention. Most of it was "doctor-talk," and far above my level of understanding.

"When he first wakes up he may be scared, but it will all be forgotten by tomorrow," Dr. Ence assured me. "He was given a drug to induce amnesia. I doubt he will remember anything."

I felt reassured, and as Matthew's hospital bed came into view I was anxious to go to him. I could find out later what the problem was...right now, I needed to see my baby.

Matthew looked small and vulnerable as he slept. Nurses came in frequently to check on his progress. One was especially attentive, and said she had kept him in the first recovery room longer than usual, "in light of what he's been through today." For some reason, her remark didn't register in my mind until months later, as pieces of the puzzle began to form a complete picture.

Matthew's recovery was phenomenal, to say the slightest. Naturally we assumed it was due to his getting more rest without apnea depriving him of the deep REM sleep he needed. I thought I had been given a new child. His personality changed completely. He quit fighting with Jordan, his five-year-old brother. He stopped all the crazy, daredevil things he was famous for in the shopping mall, grocery store, neighborhood and church. Rushes to the emergency room ceased. He quit taking naps cold turkey, and woke up early each morning; something he had never before done on his own. Most remarkable of all to Eric and me, Matthew slept in his own bed all night, every night.

We praised Dr. Ence's great work, giving him all the credit.

Then one night in April, shortly before Matthew's fourth birthday, we got the shock of our lives.

It was a Monday night, and we'd all finished a fun Family Home Evening. Eric called everyone up for prayer, as usual, in the little boy's bedroom. Jordan was in the top bunk, and Matthew was on the bottom. David and Rachel were on their way upstairs.

As I tucked Matthew's covers around him and threw fifteen-odd stuffed toys out of the way, he smiled gently and looked into my eyes.

"Mom," he said in his quiet, lisping voice. "I need to tell you about my 'thurgery.'"

"Sure, honey," I said without a thought, pulling Winnie-the-Pooh out from under his pillow.

He stroked my hand gently, as if it were a baby bunny.

"I need to tell you," he said, looking deeply and directly into my eyes, "about when I died."

I jumped up so fast I bumped my head on the top bunk.

"You didn't die!" I blurted, suddenly curious about Dr. Ence's explanation of certain "complications".

"Ye'th, I did," he insisted. "I died, and I need to tell you..."

Oh, bother. I'm getting ahead of myself. Perhaps I should start where it began, in San Jose, in June of 1991...

*Grandma LaRue with newborn twins at
Good Samaritan Hospital. April 29, 1991*

CHAPTER 2

A Full and Happy Home

"**K**jirstin, your Visiting Teachers are here," my sister, Jill, called from my entry hall. "Shall I have them sit down?" Jill's voice awakened me from a state of joyful half-sleep. I smiled at the contented faces of Matthew and Benjamin, my newborn twins, fat and happy from their nursing. Matthew's little mouth was still moving as he nursed in his dreams. Life was good.

Like most "Silicon Valley" families, we were a bit cramped in our small tract home in San Jose, California. David, our oldest at ten, shared a room with 22 month old Jordan. This was not ideal, but we hadn't been able to find a home that suited both our needs and our financial position. Eight-year-old Rachel, our only daughter, had her own room, but it was really little more than an attic sewing room. She had given up her sunny bedroom so the twins could be downstairs near my husband, Eric, and me. Rachel didn't enjoy being alone upstairs, and though it was fine right now in June, come January I knew she'd be shivering.

"Kjirstin," Jill's voice jarred me back to the present. "Shall I make your Visiting Teachers stay out on the front porch all day?"

"Of course not," I called to her. "I'm in my usual position and not about to move. Send them back."

Sheri Skiba and Kathy Callanta tiptoed down the wide, carpeted hallway into my bedroom.

The boys were stirring, and I watched as one blue eye tentatively opened to see if the ruckus was worth his waking up. It evidently wasn't, as he slowly closed it, leaving a row of tiny blond lashes in its place. All my children were blue-eyed blondes, and bald as chick-peas until their second birthdays. Our own light coloring and Scandinavian ancestry on both sides made any other possibility remote. Still, Ben showed some promise of red hair, and we watched him eagerly, hoping for a crop to sprout and appease his red-headed grandma.

"Oh, they're growing so fast!" Sheri exclaimed. "How do you ever manage twins?"

"Delegation," I answered. "Which one do you want to burp?"

Sheri grabbed Benjamin, and Kathy wailed, "Why do I always get stuck with Matthew? He never burps for me."

"He never burps for anyone without a major workout", I said. "A day or two after he was born we were still in the hospital and he started making odd faces and noises. He scared me! I'd had five children, and I'd never seen such a thing. He frightened me so badly I ran out into the hall with him, screaming for a nurse."

"Gosh," said Kathy. "What happened?"

"She whisked him off to the nursery," I said. "A few minutes later she returned and said, 'He belched like a sailor, and then he was fine.' Now we just call him 'The Sailor'."

A knock on my bedroom door stifled our laughter.

"May I come in?" Jill asked.

"Sure," I answered. "There's always room for Jill-O!"

Meeting Jill and learning she is my sister was usually a shock to most people. While I am somewhat crass, obnoxious, and nosy, Jill is always humble, loving, and fun. I give headaches; Jill gets them. My metabolism allows me to eat anything I like without gaining an ounce, but if Jill happens to smell a chocolate, she gains weight. Her hazel eyes sparkle with warmth, a contrast to my cold steel-blue eyes. Her hair, so blond in our youth, has darkened to a chestnut-colored brown and is worn in a short style. In deference to Eric's romantic preference, my blond locks nearly reached my waist.

In the past, Jill had only been able to take a short vacation with us during Christmas. Now she had eight days remaining from the ten she planned to spend here. It was wonderful to have her back in California, where we all felt she belonged.

"Kjirstin said you work in New York," Sheri said. "What do you do there?"

"I'm a Residence Hall Director in a co-ed dormitory at The State University of New York in Oswego," Jill replied. "Basically, I help six hundred students get through the trauma of college living."

"This won't be much of a vacation for you then," Sheri said with a laugh.

"Oh, I love kids," Jill said. "Especially babies. Do you have any children?"

"Yes," Sheri answered. "But none of mine were this big and strong at six weeks. I still can't believe they were twins."

"Oh, you'd believe it if you had to get up with them at night as many times as I do," I complained.

"Sheri's had plenty of practice at that game," Kathy said, sticking up for her companion. "Her kids woke everybody in the house."

"Yeah, but it wasn't because they'd cry," Sheri explained. "My children slept so soundly they'd forget to breathe. All of them had to wear a device from the hospital called an 'apnea monitor'. When their heartbeats were too slow or if they quit breathing, the monitor would go off loudly enough to wake half the neighborhood."

"How awful," I said. "I've read about apnea, but I never realized you had to deal with it. How often did the monitor go off?"

"Some nights I couldn't even count," Sheri said, "but I got used to it."

"Oh, I could never get used to that," I said. "When my sleep is interrupted I'm like a Zombie the next day. I had no idea your family had been through so much. Your one son has an artificial leg, right?"

"Oh, yeah," said Sheri, "but he has the right attitude about it. He goes around to all the elementary schools and takes his outgrown prosthesis to show how much he's grown. The kids all get a "hands-on" Show & Tell. It takes the 'fear of the unknown' out of it."

"Tell her about what he did when that gang of bullies was after him," Kathy prodded.

"Naw, she doesn't want to hear about that," Sheri said, blushing a bright shade of red, making her hair seem an even lighter blond.

"Sure she does," Kathy continued. "They were walking home from school, and these big bullies, who didn't know he had an artificial leg, were making fun of him and some other little kids..."

"Okay, okay, I'll tell her," Sheri went on. "The gang wanted to fight, so Brandan took off his leg. They were so shocked, they screamed and ran away. They never bothered them again."

We all laughed.

"What a great kid," Jill said. "Some university students I know could do better with an attitude like his. It just proves he has great parents."

"Oh, we're trying," Sheri said. "It's hard sometimes."

"Our family has been so blessed," I said. "We have a great marriage, our children are healthy and good kids most of the time. I was so afraid Benjamin would be too small to survive, especially since they were born over a month early, but Matthew weighed six pounds ten ounces and Ben was only two ounces less. He even had a better hospital APGAR score then Matthew—a perfect "10" His pediatrician said she never gives 10's, especially for the first five minutes, but Benjamin was absolutely perfect, so she had to...I even got to hold Ben before Matthew."

"She doesn't sound like a proud Mother or anything, does she?" Jill mercifully interrupted, before I had bragged too much more.

Her ribbing didn't bother me. I was a proud Mother, but also a thankful one. I knew these blessings were profound, and I felt I whispered a prayer of thanks each time I took a breath.

"I only mean," I tried to explain, "that my life is so wonderful. We've never had to face any terrible trials or sadness."

"Knock on wood," Kathy warned, rapping her knuckles on my large oak dresser. "You don't want to jinx yourself."

"Don't be silly, Kathy," I said. "Mormon's aren't superstitious."

"We all have to face trials in this life," Sheri said. "Which brings us to our Visiting Teaching Message for today..."

Emily, Rachel, Jane and Ashley Unter hold Matthew and Benjamin. June, 1991

CHAPTER 3

Of Stars and Planets

"Thanks, Jill," I called later that day, stumbling through the doorway with a package. "I'm exhausted, but it was terrific to get out of the house."

"Yeah," my husband Eric said. "Even if all we did was shop for baby toys."

"Oh, what did you get," Rachel and David shouted, jumping with excitement. "What did you get?"

Jordan joined the chorus asking, "Det? Det?" even though he'd helped to pick it out. Now 22 months old, Jordy was eager to use his newly acquired words at every opportunity. Though he was still a little guy, he had become one of the big kids seemingly overnight. "People who work with Daddy got us a gift certificate, and we found this cute mobile." I said, showing it off as the children chorused an assortment of "oohs" and "ahhs."

"After we move, we'll go back and use the rest of the gift certificate on a wagon for the little boys. I can't wait to see David pulling my 'Three Little Bears' around in it."

"Great," David groaned. "I'll have to be your slave boy, doing all the hard work."

"That's what ten-year-olds are for," Eric teased. "Like a dog sled team; 'mush-mush'," he said, pretending to crack a whip.

"Oh, I'd love to pull them around in a shiny new red wagon," Rachel volunteered. Willing eight-year-olds were certainly a blessing to have around the home.

Hurrying in to nurse and change the babies before dinner, I was glad to have a chance to put the mobile up. I chastised myself for not getting one sooner. They needed visual stimulation and it seemed they had to wait for everything just because I couldn't catch up.

Matthew and Benjamin both stared at the mobile. It was impossible to detect whether they liked it. A string of miniature Christmas lights swung above their crib. They were lit even during the day to help the twins' focus on something interesting. I didn't want them to be mentally disadvantaged simply because they didn't have my undivided attention or because they'd have to share everything.

We were sitting down to eat when I remembered to turn off the light in the hall. I glanced in the nursery at the babies and saw Benjamin vomit violently. He could have aspirated his entire feeding back into his lungs, but I grabbed him instantly and instinctively cleared his airway. In my haste, the mobile was flung across the room, but Ben was fine.

"He would have choked to death if I hadn't been right here," I thought. The realization disturbed me a lot. How could I possibly be everywhere I needed to be? Would I be able to be there for all of my children whenever they needed me? I would have been eating, not twenty feet away, and I'd never have heard him choke.

For years I'd had a running battle with my mother, a firm advocate of putting babies on their tummies to avoid the possibility of choking. She had raised five children, sleeping every one flat on their stomachs. I never understood where the feeling originated, but all my life I'd had a nearly paranoid fear of putting babies face down. All of the many pediatricians we'd had over the years said it made no difference, other than a temporary bald or flat place on the head of those sleeping on their backs. My children had all slept on their backs or sides and been fine. Now I worried, wondering if perhaps my mom was right.

I forced the worries from my mind and walked to the dining room.

At the dinner table I noticed a phenomenon not often realized in our family.

"Hey," I remarked. "What is this? A Friday night and my whole family is here? Aren't any of your friends sleeping over?"

"Nope," David answered. "We kind of thought it was like 'family time' because Aunt Jill is visiting."

"It's a miracle!" Eric remarked, imitating Curly Howard of *The Three Stooges* in his silly, cartoon-like voice. Everyone laughed. Some of us even lost the bite we'd just taken.

In an attempt to restore calm, I asked Jill how she liked being a mom for the afternoon.

"You don't get to sit down very much with twins, do you?" Jill said. "I was a little bit scared something would happen...I mean...I just finished my Red Cross Certification for CPR on Tuesday, and we concluded with infant CPR, so I wasn't too worried, but what if something happened to both of them at the same time?"

"Welcome to Motherhood," I said, smiling.
After dinner, David and Rachel cleared off the table. Jill stacked the dishes in the dishwasher and cleaned up the kitchen.

"It's still light out," Jill observed after she had finished. "Let's take the babies outside."

Benjamin seemed to sense that we were going out, and kicked happily as I bundled him together with Matthew into one baby quilt and scooped them out of the crib. My back ached as I reached the front hall. "This is the last time I'm carrying you both together,"

I groaned. "You're much too heavy for me!"

Jill arranged the babies on the quilt and I ran back inside for the second quilt. A slight breeze was blowing. It was a warm breeze, but a breeze nonetheless. A mother couldn't be too careful.

"What beautiful quilts," Jill remarked. "Did you make them?"

"No, they were made by my Relief Society sisters. I got them at the baby shower they gave me Tuesday night."

"How sweet of them."

"They made so many nice things; bibs, quilts, sleepers. One sister, Julia Hatch, drew animals that spelled out their names. She even called to ask what colors I'd decorated the nursery. By that evening she had the pictures framed and wrapped in paper she had decorated herself. It was so pretty I didn't want to open them. Julia has a new baby herself and is also the Primary President. I know she didn't have a minute to spare."

"You certainly have caring friends in your ward."

"I know that now," I said. "It took me a long time to feel a part of the group, but since they've all been sort-of forced to serve me, and I was forced to accept their service, I finally feel like I'm starting to belong. You know, they even bought me two new car seats for the babies?"

"That's great."

"I couldn't believe it. We'll be moving out of the ward soon, and still they've given me all they could. I don't know if I'll ever be able to repay them in time or service, and now even financially."

"I don't think they expect you to repay them, Kjirstin."

"When we first moved to the valley, a woman from church watched my kids one day when I really needed a break. I wanted to pay her, or repay her, but she said, "Do it for someone else sometime; that will pay me back.""

"That's as it should be," Jill said. "Imagine how the world would be if everyone had that attitude."

The moon was a slender sliver of pale yellow, and the lights of

Mars, Venus and Jupiter were all visible beside it; an unusual planetary alignment in force for the first time in three hundred years. Looking up, I felt awed, and blessed to be able to see it so clearly and to share it all with my sister.

We chatted about her work, my future plans, and how Eric and I had decided the children's names.

Both babies were wide awake. They seemed to enjoy the breeze and different surroundings.

Looking at my baby boys, I was again in awe. After back surgery at the age of twenty-three, the doctor said I would never be able to have children. The Lord had blessed me with five miracles. These two were my crowning achievement. I could hardly wait to send my orthopedic surgeon a Christmas Card with our annual family photograph attached.

Though fraternal, the boys looked so much alike I hadn't dared to remove the wrist bracelet until they were a month old. The only way I could tell them apart was by their nursing habits. Ben loved to nurse. I looked at him and smiled, but he didn't smile back.

"Aw, c'mon," I coaxed. "Gimme smile. Give Momma a smile."

"He smiled at me last night," Jill said proudly.

"I know!" I said. "We all saw that smile. It was so big I recorded it on his baby calendar. In fact, I think Benjamin has smiled at everybody. Maffy is going to have to work hard to catch up to my little Benzie."

"Watch it," Jill warned. "You're playing favorites."

"Oh, I know." I said, gasping a bit at being caught. "Isn't it terrible? Five children and I've never even been tempted to have a favorite until Benjamin."

"He is pretty special, isn't he?" She asked. "Why? What is it about him?"

"I don't know, and yet, I feel I've always known..." my voice was lost in the warm June breeze, but something churned within me. A fear? A memory? "I had quite a struggle bonding to him. I held him emotionally at arms length because I didn't want to love him and lose him and be hurt, but once I accepted that he actually was healthy, I let go of my fear. He's so perfect. I love him right now more than anything or anyone."

Matthew was asleep, snuggled warmly into his new quilt on the fresh, green lawn his big brother, David, had mowed earlier in the day. Benjamin stared up at me, as if commanding me to look deeply into his cobalt blue eyes.

Ben continued to stare. His eyes held me as if suspended in time. How could a newborn baby have eyes as those I'd only seen on elderly men who had learned all the lessons of life? They were filled with more than the intelligence I had seen in the others; I can only call it wisdom. He did not release his visual grip on me. He didn't look away.

"This is not possible," I told myself. *"A newborn baby has a very short attention span...they break it off and move on to something more interesting..."*

"Kjirstin," Jill remarked. "He hasn't taken his eyes off you for three or four minutes!"

Again, a fear stirred deep inside me; a fear from long ago; a fear I couldn't remember, and yet knew as if I'd rehearsed it a hundred times on some far-away stage.

"Those hedges are driving me crazy," I said, forcefully breaking Ben's gaze by jumping up. "I'm going to prune them before it's completely dark."

Jill rearranged the babies and snapped some photos.

"It's too dark to take pictures," I called from behind the bottle brush hedge. "We'll have plenty of light tomorrow. Don't waste your film."

"Okay." Jill answered, but I saw another flash.

"Same old sis," I thought.

"Darn!" I hollered. "I forgot...I have a coupon...I was going to take all the kids to the photo studio today to get a picture taken of them for Eric for Father's Day."

"You're a photographer," Jill said. "You can take it yourself."

"Ha!" I laughed. "You know, 'and the cobbler's kids have no shoes'. I still don't have a family portrait with all of us in it."

"You're kidding!"

"Well, I've been waiting for everyone to be here together, and the babies skin to clear up, and Rachel and I to have our hair looking nice on the same day."

"It will never happen."

"I know...will you take a picture of us after church on Sunday?"

"Sure," Jill promised.

"Tomorrow is June 15th," I said, shoving the pruned branches into garbage cans. "I turned down a wedding for that day. I could have shot it if I'd known I'd have the babies April 29th instead of the end of May...and if I'd known *you'd* be here to baby-sit!"

"Dream it."

"Well, I guess my hands are rather full these days."

It was too dark to pick up all the pieces of the bottle brush hedge, but I got the big ones. Out on the driveway were two large piles of stone and tan bark, waiting for us to finish off our landscaping project. Tomorrow would be a busy day.

Benjamin and Matthew were soundly sleeping. It was time to go inside.

*Jordan, 20 months, with Matthew
and Benjamin. May, 1991*

CHAPTER 4

Nightmare at Dawn

Benjamin nursed well, as usual, and fell quickly into dreamland. Matthew, as usual, fussed a lot and bit me. I finally gave him a bottle, but he was up again at eleven, twelve-thirty, and two o'clock.

By two-thirty I was worried. Matthew seemed very congested and would not settle down. I got out two different medical books, and both said to call the doctor. After five children I felt I could handle a little cold, and we decided not to wake up the doctor. Eric and I took turns walking the halls with him. Eric didn't think we needed to call the doctor either, but I was concerned, so we prayed about it and felt reassured that Matthew would be okay.

Benjamin was sleeping so soundly he didn't even wake up by three for his feeding. He was such a good baby. He'd slept all night twice before he was a month old.

By four-thirty I was exhausted. Matthew and I had been up nearly the whole night, and I knew Benjamin would wake up for his feeding at any moment. As I nursed Matthew, I felt him finally settle down, and his breathing seemed clearer.

One of the medical books had suggested laying him at a thirty degree angle. As we finished nursing, I decided to get the bedrest, an overstuffed pillow. It would make a suitable wedge if I laid it down, and propped him up on it.

"Put Ben up next to him," I heard the still, small voice whisper.

"Yes," I thought numbly. *"That's a good idea. I'll do that."*

"Put Ben up next to him," I heard again, and again I promised, "Yes, I will."

"What?" Eric asked, stirring beside me.

I hadn't realized that I'd actually answered out loud, and I reassured Eric that everything was fine.

Matthew slept soundly against my shoulder as I carefully bent down to get the bedrest from the foot of my bed.

I tiptoed into the nursery. Barely daring to breathe lest I awaken either of them, I put the bedrest upside down on the mattress. It created a respectable incline on which I placed Matthew.

The vaporizer coughed out its steady stream of warm white mist that actually did seem to help the babies breathe. I scooted Matthew over to the left side of the pillow, making room to prop Benjamin up beside him, on the right.

Benjamin was comfortably snuggled down on his tummy in the natural sheepskin we had bought in Scotland. A cotton diaper was tucked under his soft face, and his head was snuggled in the latest device for keeping babies comfortable. I could hear his regular, steady breathing.

"I guess Mom was right," I thought. *"Benjamin really does sleep better on his stomach."*

Reaching for him, he stirred, and I could sense that he was close to waking up.

"If he wakes up, he'll be hungry, and I've just nursed Matthew," I considered. *"I'm so tired...'let sleeping babes lie,' they always say. Maybe*

I shouldn't disturb him right now. I'll go back to bed and get a little sleep. He'll be awake in a half-hour at the most. Then I'll have enough milk to nurse him and I'll move him next to Matthew."

The sky was beginning to turn from blue to the pinky-gray of early morning. I was asleep before I could even appreciate my warm bed.

* * *

My eyes opened to a room filled with yellow sunshine and the prattle of Jordan in the nursery, tormenting the twins.

"No!" was my first thought as fear seized every nerve in my body. *"It's been too long!"*

Wide awake, I jumped straight out of bed and nearly flew into the nursery.

Jordan was poking at Matthew through the crib bars, and I smiled gently but uneasily at him, pushing him aside as my eyes searched for Ben.

All I could see was a three inch circle of the back of his head. Even with the curtains closed, I knew. It was white. Too white.

It was the nightmare I'd had weeks before, when I woke from a dream that Ben had died. Then, Eric had held me and said, *"Honey, it was just a dream, everything is fine,"* but it was real this time. Everything wasn't fine, and I knew absolutely that nothing would ever really be fine again.

I could hear a loud and horrible low-pitched, grating, moan. It was coming from deep inside me, and I couldn't control it.

Moaning and crying, I grabbed him up. "Ben! No! Not my Ben! Not my Baby Ben!"

His eyes were closed, and a deep blue bruise seemed to outline them. His tiny body was solid and floppy, but it was still warm. I hoped. I prayed.

"9-1-1! 9-1-1!" I screamed, running for the phone.

David jumped off his bunk bed asking, "What? What's wrong?"

Eric, half-asleep from the long ordeal the night before, stumbled out of our room. He and David saw Ben at the same time.

"Matthew?" Eric asked.

"No, Ben! It's Ben!" I wailed. "It's my Baby Ben." I handed him to Eric as I waited impatiently for the emergency line to answer. "But Matthew is sick, not Ben..." Eric muttered, trying to make sense of the situation as he began blowing air into Ben's mouth.

Jill and Rachel were racing down the stairs.

"CPR! CPR!," I shouted to Jill as a woman answered the emergency line.

Somehow I managed to communicate our situation to the dispatcher and she assured me that help was on the way.

Jill had Ben on the living room table, and was administering mouth to mouth resuscitation. We gathered the children and knelt in a circle. We prayed aloud; first me, and then Eric.

After the prayer I called Bruce Kusch, our bishop. He asked if I had called 9-1-1, and then he said, "I can hear the ambulance coming now."

I grabbed a robe for Eric and put on my own, then raced to the front yard.

A policeman was jumping out of his patrol car. He put his donut down first, dusting its sugar specks from the tummy section of his navy blue wool uniform. In any other circumstance, I'm sure I would have laughed. I pointed to my front door and shouted, "In there...please hurry." And he did.

By then people were gathering, and I was trying hard to stay in control, but I couldn't manage it. Neighbors came from up and down the block, and held me and cried with me and prayed aloud for Benjamin.

Two fire trucks arrived, their fluorescent chartreuse a vivid contrast to the dark events of the morning.

Our sidewalk was filled with curious and concerned neighbors who had suddenly and forever become friends.

An ambulance stopped in the middle of the street and two

paramedics raced inside.

Linda Browne, our Relief Society President, arrived and I broke down. "It's Ben, Linda...I knew it...I told you...he's dying. He's going to die..."

She took me by my shoulders and shook me; hard.

"Get a grip," she ordered. "You can't give up now. Ben needs your faith. You've got to believe."

I nodded my head. She was right, and I knew I needed to continue the prayers in my heart on his behalf; believing he could be healed if it was truly the Lord's will. It meant so much to me to have her there, holding me. From the tears in her eyes I knew she cared. I could feel her love for me, and for Benjamin.

"Thank you, Linda." I said, hugging her tightly. "Thanks for being here when I need you."

Bishop Kusch arrived and led us into the house. I couldn't bear to watch the rescue efforts. I wandered in and out of the house. Someone said I had to get dressed and go to the hospital. My neighbor, Denise, took me into my room and helped me find a dress. It was a new multicolored cotton skirt and blouse that I'd worn to the baby shower four days before. I put it on knowing I'd never wear it again.

Denise took Jordan to her house and Jill stayed home to watch the other children.

Bishop Kusch drove Eric and me the few blocks to the hospital. I'd always felt safe, living so close to a hospital. Now I prayed it would be close enough to make a difference.

Jordy, 18 months old, in the aquarium
(I had to grab my camera before
rescuing him) February, 1991

CHAPTER 5

Reflections of Hope

M y mind wandered back to the past few months as I'd stayed in bed on doctor's orders to hopefully delay an early delivery of the twins. They'd needed every hour they spent developing in my bulging womb. Had I rested enough? Was it my fault he was on his way to the hospital? Was it because I hadn't asked people to help me? Was it due to the sheepskin he'd slept on, or my own pride?

Close friends were something I hadn't had since grade school. I guarded against becoming close to anyone with the justification that eventually I'd move or they would. It didn't seem wise to make friends I couldn't keep. I became a master at smiling big, acting friendly, and never getting to know anyone on a personal level.

After Eric and I married, our first ten years were spent on the move. We lived in nine different homes in seven different cities and three different countries. His Time and Frequency engineering career with Hewlett-Packard often sent us packing. Our first two children circled the globe twice before Rachel turned five.

We finally settled down in the San Jose 15th Ward. As soon as I began to feel comfortable, the boundary lines of the ward were changed, and we found ourselves in the 24th Ward without even moving. My first weeks in the new ward weren't easy. We planned to stay here forever, so for the first time in my life, I let go. My naturally gregarious feelings overflowed as I walked up to people as if we were old friends in my rush to get acquainted. Of course they considered me pushy and turned their backs on me. Literally.

What I didn't understand at the time was that the 24th Ward members were all suffering from losing half of their old friends. Like me, they were having a hard time coping. I felt like the "new" one in the crowd. It didn't enter my mind that the other half of the 15th Ward who came in with me, was also new to them. Many who feared making friends of strangers and learning all the new names had simply retreated with their comfortable old friends.

Fault-finding came easily for me, and I found myself wishing my family could have church by ourselves.

Sacrament meeting speakers seemed to include the same four men every week. They also seemed to speak on the same four subjects. I tried not to complain, but was grateful to have a young child who needed frequent "foyer control." I noticed my husband and I would both readily volunteer to take him out into the chapel's foyer, rather than sit through what felt like the same meeting we'd endured the week before.

One man we found particularly offensive actually offered the opening prayer in which he said, "Thank you, Heavenly Father, for making me so good and so humble."

We reminded ourselves that ours is a church of lay-persons, and nobody is paid for their services, so we shouldn't complain. We are all here to learn. Though we found his "I's" and "me's" abhorrent it taught us to remember not to make the same mistake if we are ever called upon to pray in a meeting intended for the entire congregation.

On another Sunday, a woman got up to speak. Her son was leaving on his mission. She gave one of the most beautiful, spiritually uplifting talks I had ever heard. I was shocked at her words as she concluded, "I have been a member of this ward for fourteen years," she said, "and this is the first time I've ever been asked to speak in Sacrament Meeting, so I apologize for being so nervous."

Eric and I exchanged glances of astonishment, incomprehension, and sadness. How could such a vast resource of human excellence remain untapped by so many different ward leaders for fourteen years?

During a Fast and Testimony meeting shortly after we were placed in the 24th Ward through the boundary change, I, in my usual tactless manner, had blurted, "I've been to LDS Wards all over the world, and this is by far the most unfriendly ward I've ever attended."

Several people approached me after the meeting and agreed with me, some thanking me for voicing what they could not say. I felt smug in my "inspiration," and certain my words would help change attitudes to a more positive vein.

For the first two weeks after my infamous "testimony," I was greeted with large smiles and pats on the back. People went out of their way to say "hello" and inquire after my health. Soon I realized that this patronage was far worse than being ignored. I felt like the toothless first-grader at Christmas time, besieged by people exclaiming, "Bet I know what you want for Christmas...your two front teeth!" Though the ward members were sickeningly sweet to me, they continued to ignore visitors, and moved from their seats if someone they didn't feel comfortable around sat beside them. My words had done nothing to help change that condition, and my smiles for strangers were not infectious enough to prompt them to visit a second time. Somewhere in my mind, the old adage about getting more bees with honey than salt simmered, but I couldn't bring it to a boil. I felt doomed to live in a ward of strangers.

Like many people, I suffer from the "I can handle it" syndrome.

Pile it on. Higher and deeper. I can do everything all by myself. With my fourth pregnancy well on it's way, it soon became obvious I could not do anything.

One afternoon the recently called Relief Society President came to my home. Linda Browne is a short, smiling, likable and caring woman. She'd had her share of trouble when her husband recovered from an illness that was usually terminal. It had made her as tough as a turtle's shell, and just as soft as one on the inside.

We sat across from each other at my breakfast table. I moved the bills and newspapers aside, scraping as much dried yogurt from her place as I could before breaking the news.

"Do you know if it's going to be a boy or a girl yet?" She'd asked that warm day in early December.

"Probably both," I said.

"Very funny," she said, trying to laugh it off, but not moving her eyes from mine.

"Notice I'm not laughing," I said.

"Kjirstin," she wailed. "You're not having twins!"

"I'm not?" I teased, showing her the ultrasound photograph featuring "Twin A" and "Twin B".

We both screamed and laughed and cried together that day. Twins are just such a shock. Even when you're expecting them.

Linda knew I was barely holding on as it was with the energy I expended on Jordan, then sixteen months old. She knew the Relief Society would have it's work cut out. At that moment I was determined not to ask for help. Someone else could be a service project. Even with twins on the way, I was resistant to any sort of change in my usual routine. Somehow I still thought I could continue to be a room mother to both of my older children, volunteer for a dozen different projects, enjoy my photography club, and cook gourmet meals. I promised myself I'd slow down after they were born.

Two months later, ordered by my doctor to have complete bed rest, my pride was forced to fly out the window.

A prisoner in my own bed, I'd spent those first two February days watching 18-month-old Jordan run in circles around my room and up and over my 44 inch belly.

"Jordy," I begged. "Lie down here beside mommy and read this book."

He'd look at me as if I were speaking Chinese, and then he'd go swing on the drapes. Once I had to fish him out of the aquarium. It was on top of David's forty inch tall dresser, but somehow, he had climbed up there and was standing in it.

All I could do was watch as all semblance of an organized home crumbled around me.

Reinforcements arrived in the form of Jane Unter and her friend Debra Howard. The Unter's had been friends since we first arrived in San Jose. Jane stayed with me at the hospital during my labor with Jordan. She helped David and Rachel, who were also present in the delivery room, to better understand the birth process. Debra had been confined to bed herself, and when Jane asked her what she should do to help me, Debra wasted no time. Though not a member of our church, she knew all about service. "Go clean her house!" She'd commanded. Both women arrived at my home early one Saturday, armed with mops and cleanser. They worked without a break, going home at dinner time leaving a hot meal prepared for my family and a battle plan for my husband. Their selfless acts melted my pride, and I finally realized I couldn't do much of anything by myself for awhile.

Linda Browne was called into action. She arranged meals and assigned Visiting Teachers who could handle my many child care, housekeeping and shopping needs.

She called Sheri Skiba as my new Visiting Teacher. I was very grumpy about it at first. I liked my former Visiting Teacher, who already knew what a rotten housekeeper I was, so she was prepared. I didn't want to force a new Visiting Teacher to fight her way past my sticky children to clean up my messy kitchen. Linda Browne said she'd felt "prompted" to call Sheri, so reluctantly, I agreed.

In early February, my insurance agent called to ask if I could shoot his daughter's wedding on the 15th of June. I had photographed another daughter's wedding a few year's earlier, and they wanted me again. I was pleased to know how well they liked my work. Shooting weddings was my favorite thing to do. I had never turned one down no matter how far I had to drive, or if my temperature was 103 degrees, or if I was nursing a baby. (Though I must admit it was probably mostly for the wedding cake.) I had always managed to "do it all" and fully expected to continue after the babies were born.

The twins were due May 25th. *"Sure,"* I thought. *"Twins are usually early. I can do it. No problem."* I started asking the usual questions: Did they want photos at the temple? How many attendants would they have? Would they need an engagement picture taken before the wedding?

A small voice then whispered, *"Say 'no', Kjirstin. You'll be busy that day. Just say you're sorry, but you really can't do it that day."* I heard myself turning down the job, and I was stunned.

Now it was starting to make sense. *I'm on my way to the hospital—I couldn't possibly work today. My baby needs me; but how did I know I'd have to turn down today's wedding nearly five months ago when my agent first called? How did I know?*

Why did it make sense? It didn't. It couldn't. I couldn't possibly have known, and yet I did! Again I felt as if I were on a stage, acting out a play, but not a play; more like a lifetime plan...something designed to happen exactly as it did...but over which I had no real control. I was an actor. I knew my lines, and I knew the plot, but who was directing? Was the Lord's plan so structured that He knew the beginning and the end because they had already happened? Had I seen it? Did I *really* know? Why didn't I do something to stop it from happening? Couldn't I have done something to prevent it?

I forced the thoughts from my mind. They were too disturbing.

I tried to concentrate on something else.

Why did being a mother have to be so hard? I thought of my own mother, and how she had helped me through the years. She was always there for me; not always with what I felt I needed, but with plenty of suggestions for help.

My mother quit her job to come to stay with us the weeks before the twins were born. She took over so completely, she refused a minute for herself. Mom hurt her knee running upstairs too many times, and we realized we were asking far too much of her. She had already raised five children. A young widow with her own life to lead, she didn't need to feel obligated to raise five more. When the twins were three weeks old, she returned to her home in Victorville.

Eric took as much time off his work as he dared. Engineers were being laid-off all over the country, and though his job seemed secure, he didn't want to give anyone an excuse to dispose of him.

David and Rachel were called upon to perform many more chores around the house, and I counted on them to help keep Jordan occupied. We hired Heather, a young English girl, to handle all the extra housework. She was a wonderful companion for me, and her hard work permitted me to have time to know and love my little babies. She worked many extra hours without pay, and became like a member of our family.

Each person touching our life played a role in helping us discover the joy in raising and loving our little family. Most nights and mornings as we'd gather for prayer, I paused to look at each face, and thank my Heavenly Father for sending me such wonderful people to love. I knew they loved me with equal intensity. In life, there are no greater rewards.

Bishop Kusch drove as fast as he could to try to keep up with the ambulance.

"Please," I prayed silently. "Please..." but I couldn't find words to finish my plea.

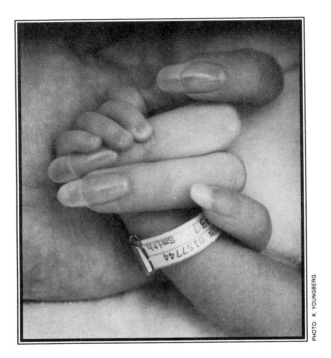

Friday, May 3, 1991
Benjamin's hand in mine

CHAPTER 6

Thy Will Be Done

We parked the car and bolted for the emergency room, but I stopped by the ambulance. *Hadn't it arrived just seconds before us? Where were the doctors? Why weren't they rushing my baby into the hospital?* When I voiced these fears aloud, Eric and Bishop Kusch led me gently inside.

"They know what they're doing...it's not always like you see it in the movies."

Suddenly everything seemed to swim in a whirlpool of green. I felt myself sinking to my knees, and I wanted desperately to pray. I groped for a chair, but a nurse came and took us from the waiting room to a dark little cubbyhole with a bed, cleaning supplies, and dozens of coats, purses, and brown-bag lunches.

They don't want a hysterical woman disturbing their peaceful waiting room, I thought, vaguely conscious of the scene I must be making. I tried to pull myself together, to be a strength for my husband who struggled as I did with feelings we couldn't begin to comprehend.

A nurse explained what was going on, but I was unable to understand any of it.

"Is he breathing yet?" I asked.

"A machine is breathing for him," she answered.

"Good," I nodded. "That's good."

It wasn't good, and I knew it. I managed to look at Eric for the first time all morning. He looked as if he wanted to protect me from the pain we both felt, and I realized I was trying to do the same for him.

Most of our communicating occurred without words. We faced each other and held on to each other, both supporting, and being supported. We both knew what had to be done, but neither of us could speak the words.

Eric mercifully took over.

"We have to pray that our Heavenly Father's will be done," he managed to say.

"No," I cried. "I can't. I can't."

We searched each others tear-filled eyes for answers, help, relief. We cried together, and found ourselves again on our knees, with Bishop Kusch, not much older than we are, acting well his part as the father of our ward. We drew upon his strength, and voiced the prayer we knew we must.

"..and Father, we ask that Benjamin will be restored to full health...but trusting in Thy knowledge of things we cannot see, we ask that Thy will be done..."

Beeping noises I had not been aware of before, now stopped. A large metal door opened and closed. I heard the shuffling noise of cloth-garbed shoes pad softly toward our door. Two knocks and the door opened, then closed to allow us a private *"Amen."*

Bishop Kusch rose to admit the knocker, who stood stoically and uttered the words we most feared.

"I'm sorry," she said.

Tears we thought had already run dry poured unbidden.

Bishop Kusch encircled us with his arms, and I felt as if "the armies of heaven" I had often sung about were there with me. Until that moment I had never felt so great a power. We were in a tiny room, yet it was filled with all the angels in heaven. My heart was broken, but I felt the combined strength of untold millions, hundreds of millions, lifting me up.

I stopped crying and shaking, and was able to listen as a doctor came in and introduced himself. He explained that Ben had died of something called S.I.D.S.; Sudden Infant Death Syndrome, sometimes called Crib Death.

"It will probably take you a few days to understand, but please believe me when I tell you it was not your fault. S.I.D.S. dates back to Old Testament days, and with all our modern technology and understanding, it is still as mysterious today as in ancient times. It can't be predicted or prevented. There is nothing you could have done."

My head was shaking. I heard him, but I didn't believe him.

"I have been a doctor for a lot of years," he continued. "I have seen dozens of cases. If it were my own child who died in my arms while we were standing with him in the middle of the best-equipped hospital, with the finest surgical team in the world, there would be nothing we could do for him. Nothing! We can bring back drowning, choking; almost any case has been documented. Any death...except from S.I.D.S."

The nurse who had attended us earlier now asked if we would like to see Ben. She explained that he had a plastic device in his mouth and that he would feel kind of like a doll.

Bishop Kusch asked if we would like to be alone, but we knew without conferring that we wanted him to stay with us.

We walked in silence toward the emergency room.

The room seemed immense and sterile and empty. I felt as if I were viewing it through a fish-eye lens. Distorted. The walls, floor and ceiling meshing together and looming larger than life. The center small, bare and white. An operating bed covered with sheets, and one tiny body, empty too soon.

He seemed so still, so cold, so alone.

I picked him up, aware that he was no longer there, but wanting desperately to have him return.

I hated the plastic thing, and wanted to rip it out, and kiss his sweet lips one last time, but Eric reminded me gently that it had to remain in his mouth.

I cradled his tiny body in my arms. I knew it was only his shell, and that it was empty now, but I was hopelessly trying to make him warm again. It must be a mother's born instinct to keep her off-spring warm.

My favorite position had always been to lie on my back with my baby nestled between my breasts, my arms snugly wrapping him to me. In that position I had always felt the nurturer, the love-giver. He could feel my heartbeat and I could kiss his head and whisper him songs and rhymes until he'd sleep. Often we would sleep for hours together, almost as one. After the twins were born, it was even better, as Eric's chest was not left wanting, and four of us became as two and, snuggling closer, as one.

Eric did not consider it odd, then, when I climbed onto the operating bed, and laid down. Nestling Benjamin's body, I whispered my love to him. Eric stood beside me, holding my arm, and stroking Ben, while we said our good-bye's together.

I had a distinct impression that he had stayed longer with us than he was supposed to, and that it was because of our faith and prayers, and those of our friends, that he was permitted to stay longer. I thanked him. He seemed to be in a hurry to leave, but wanted to stay with us to answer our questions.

I asked him what we should do now, and felt an immediate answer.

"He wants to be buried beside your father," I said.

"I know," Eric replied.

We both felt it was time to go, and that our other children needed us.

We thanked him for the privilege of being his parents, and told him we loved him. We promised to do our best to return the entire family to the presence of our Heavenly Father, so we could live again as a family one day.

As we walked past the hospital waiting room, Linda Browne and my neighbor, Delores Rodriguez, came to offer us comfort. It was strange, but I felt as if I could comfort them.

"It's just such a shock," Delores said.

"Yes," I answered, at the same time feeling it really wasn't a shock at all. While I couldn't say I knew absolutely that Benjamin would never live a long and full life, I did have feelings all along that he was not meant to stay. Benjamin was dead, but only for this earthly existence. He was very much alive in the heavenly sphere. I had a sure knowledge of this, and I wanted to shout it to everyone I met.

PHOTO: K. YOUNGBERG

Grandmother, Jenifer, with Benjamin and Matthew. Friday, May 3, 1991

CHAPTER 7

Pieces of a Plan

As we rode home, I felt at peace; almost happy. I even managed a joke. I missed my chance," I said. "There we were, talking to someone on the other side, and I didn't even ask him what heaven looked like."

"Does it matter?" Eric asked.

Of course it didn't; I felt then that I had learned a valuable lesson about what is and is not important. Very few things truly matter.

Eric and I discussed how we would tell the older children about Benjamin. We noted how remarkable the timing seemed.

"What if I hadn't taken yesterday off?" Eric said. "I was able to spend the entire day at home with you, and get to know him better."

"I'm still amazed at how everyone was home," I said. "It was terrible, but can you imagine how David would feel if he'd been at a friend's house?"

"Rachel might have had someone sleeping overnight," Eric said. "That could have been traumatic for both of them. We were so blessed. I could have been on a business trip out of the country. It could have taken over a day just to get home to you."

"I couldn't make it without you," I said, knowing how melodramatic it must sound, yet meaning every word.

I looked out the window of the bishop's car, amazed at how normal everything appeared. People walked to the shopping center. People drove to work. Benjamin's life had stopped, but the world kept going. It didn't seem right, somehow. I wanted to shout at everything and everyone to stop. I wanted them to have a moment of silence, to cry as I cried, or to at least look sad. It seemed inappropriate that everything was the same outside, yet everything in my life had changed forever.

Bishop Kusch pulled up in front of our house.

I went next door to Denise's to get Jordan.

"He didn't make it," I told her, then cried again.

Jordy was happy to see me, but seemed a little bewildered. It was the first time he'd been to the house next door by himself. He seemed to know something was wrong as we walked slowly home.

Eric and I sat on the couch in our living room. Our children gathered solemnly around us. Jill stayed in the kitchen with Linda Browne, and Bishop Kusch stood by the wall, halfway between the two groups.

"Ben died," Eric said simply, allowing each child to assimilate the information in his own way.

"He can't be dead," Rachel cried. "We prayed, and he had a blessing!"

"Yeah," David said quietly. He looked very strained. I told him it was okay to cry. "But you and Daddy aren't crying," he sobbed at last.

"There will be lots of crying around here," Eric said. "We will all cry as much and as long as we need to cry."

We told the children how much we loved Ben, how much we wanted him to stay and grow and be a part of our family, but how that wasn't part of the eternal plan. The plan we couldn't see. The plan only our Heavenly Father knows. We bore our testimonies about the eternal plan, and reminded the older children about the Family Home Evening lesson we had before Jordan was born. We again taught them the eternal nature of our bodies, and how sometimes all a spirit needed was to gain a body, even for a little time, so he could one day be resurrected whole, in body and spirit.

"When we pray in faith, we must always remember that it is not only our desires, but what our Father in Heaven wants," Eric explained. "He knows what is best for everyone, and even though it hurts us now, we will someday understand why it was necessary for Benjamin to return to his heavenly home so soon."

I asked Bishop Kusch to read from the Scriptures, which he did, giving us all comfort and reassurance that we would see Benjamin again. He wasn't gone forever, merely for a time, and we will yet raise him as our own son and brother.

In addition to the Scriptures, I was especially comforted by the words of our first latter-day prophet, Joseph Smith: *"The Lord takes many away even in infancy, that they may escape the envy of man, and the sorrows and evils of this present world; they were too pure, too lovely, to live on this earth; therefore, if rightly considered, instead of mourning we have reason to rejoice as they are delivered from evil, and we shall have them again...The only difference between the old and the young dying is, one lives longer in heaven and eternal light and glory than the other, and is freed a little sooner from this miserable wicked world."* (Teachings of the Prophet Joseph Smith, pp.196-197.)

Also from Joseph Smith: *"Shall mothers have their children in eternity? Yes! Yes! Mothers, you shall have your children; for they shall have eternal life, for their debt is paid...but as the child dies, so shall it rise from the dead, and be forever living in the learning of God."* (Discourses of the Prophet Joseph Smith, History of the Church, Vol. VI, p.316)

I told the children I knew we would be sent a Valiant Spirit...a baby born just to gain his body, and then return to Heavenly Father. I couldn't quite remember at the time how I knew, but I did. I fully expected him to fill his lungs with that first breath of air, and then die. Months later, after reading my own journal entries, and from friends returning letters I'd written to them about my twins, (some of the letters written years before they were born), I began to recall the marvelous events surrounding the birth and death of Benjamin.

When I was pregnant I wrote letters to friends asking them to say a special prayer for Benjamin. None of the many physicians I'd visited during my pregnancy ever indicated a problem, yet I knew Ben needed extra care. I used to rub my tummy and talk to him, and I did ask him to grow strong in there, but I prepared myself for his death. When he was born so healthy, I was really surprised. I kept waiting for him to get sick or something, and when he didn't, I counted us blessed. Now I felt guilty for not preparing the children better.

"Remember in that same Family Home Evening lesson we talked about a glove?" Eric asked. "We learned about how our body is like a glove, but our hand is like our spirit. When we die, the glove, our body, remains behind. It's just a shell; it can't move without the spirit, or hand, inside of it. Our spirit, like the hand inside the glove, continues to live, to move forward into another place we can't see."

David and Rachel needed to be held and comforted, but there was very little time.

Sister Browne said we had to take Matthew to the hospital as soon as possible. The physicians needed to be sure apnea wasn't a problem for Matthew, and he would be monitored for a couple of days. I had to leave the older children's questions for Eric to answer.

All I wanted to take were my Scriptures and Journal. I moved to do the essential things, nothing more.

Matthew slept during most of the ride to Good Samaritan Hospital. It was further away than Santa Teresa Hospital, where Ben was...where Ben's body was...

Everywhere we went we had to answer questions.

"Why is Matthew being admitted?" the woman behind the desk wanted to know.

"The doctor wants to monitor him because his twin brother died of S.I.D.S. this morning," I said, amazed at my own composure.

Linda stayed and Bishop Kusch left to make arrangements for the funeral.

A nurse came in and put up a bright mobile. Matthew smiled immediately. He didn't seem to notice Benjamin was gone.

Later Eric and Bishop Kusch came to get me. We had to go to the funeral home.

I hated the mortuary. I was quite upset. I didn't want to order 'memorial folders,' 'newspaper space' or 'embalming services'. Most of all I didn't want to order Ben's casket. I didn't want to go into that room full of coffins and pick one out for my baby.

Eric had to draw upon every ounce of his patience, his strength and his covenanted eternal love to forcefully drag me into that room. I don't know which of us shed more tears. That fifteen seconds of my life was the most difficult I've ever experienced. The 7.1 Loma Prieta earthquake, just a few miles west of us, was like a party compared to these fifteen seconds.

I took one step into the room, said, "No way," and walked out. All I wanted was a simple wooden box. A small one I could carry all by myself if I had to...I didn't want quilted satin. I didn't want a fancy lace pillow, and I certainly didn't want silver pallbearer handles.

"Well," crowed the mortuary hawk, looking at me as though I'd slithered in from the wrong side of the tracks. "We do have one model, but it's not used for open-casket funerals...it's not 'dressed out' inside."

I asked to see it.

He protested, then called someone to, "bring it up from the warehouse".

"Oh, don't bother," I said sarcastically. "Where is the warehouse?

I'll walk there myself."

Eric whispered loudly through his clenched teeth, asking me to please settle down. I tried very hard to be civil.

When I saw the little white box, I knew Benjamin would be buried in it. A far cry from ideal, it would do. I knew the sooner I agreed, the sooner we'd be out of there.

They asked what Ben would wear, and I knew instantly.

I remembered staring at the sweet little white blessing outfit at the Beehive Clothing Store a few days before. It had struck me for some reason, and the woman waiting on me had asked then if I'd like to see it. I had said, "Yes," and had her take it down from the wall display so I could look it over. This was very odd, because I never ask salespeople to do anything for me. I always say, "No, thank you," and do whatever I need to do without help. I remember looking at the tiny white buttons and the cute little cap. The saleswoman even asked if I'd like it wrapped, which caused me to blush and admit that I didn't need it. My babies had already been blessed. Eric's mother, LaRue, had purchased beautiful Dior christening suits, which they had worn at their Blessing's a week earlier.

Bishop Kusch drove us to the Beehive Clothing Store. I wrote the check without saying a word, and never looked at the tiny outfit. Tears were starting to come out again, and I didn't want the saleswoman to know that our purchase was not for a happy occasion. Our bishop took us back to the hospital. Later, Linda Browne drove us home.

Jill had prepared dinner, and our home teacher was hauling stuff from our side yard to the dump. The Elder's Quorum had spread out the rocks and tan-bark. Our landscaping project had been completed by them in a few hours.

"*Why,*" I wondered, "*couldn't we do this before...everyone working together...making light work...painting and fixing...getting to know each other...why did it take a death to make people care?*"

I already knew the answer. It had been rubbed in my face when we once asked church members for help painting our house. I had in mind a quiet Saturday, with everybody pitching in to help. A yard full of babies being watched by older children, and teens and parents painting and chatting, followed by a big meal for everyone. We didn't even want it free. We suggested donating the money we would have paid a painting contractor as a fast offering or for the scouting program.

"We never do that sort of stuff in this ward—people around here have more money than time," the Elder's Quorum President had said.

My dreams of fun "getting-to-know-you" service projects were left floating in the California breeze, forever quashed.

"I called Mom," Jill announced, forcing my thoughts back to the present. "She doesn't think she can make it for Benjamin's funeral."

"What's the problem?" I snapped. "Is she going to miss a big Single's Dance?"

"No!" Jill said, close to tears. "It's...she doesn't know if...if..."

I felt like scum. How could I have forgotten? My mother had always hated funerals. More than a visit to dentist, she hated funerals, and she really hated dentists.

I realized how much of this my sister had taken upon herself. Jill had stayed home comforting David and Rachel all day, and made all the phone calls to family and friends. She cleaned house, cooked, and kept Jordan out of mischief and in clean diapers, leaving Eric free to make funeral arrangements and sort through his grief.

Jill had always been like that-the good girl-the fixer. She invariably seemed to know what was needed, and was never too shy to pitch in and do it.

Though Jill wants more than anything else to be married and surrounded by her own children, she knows she will probably be single her whole life on earth. She seems peacefully resigned to her unmarried state. I find myself wishing I could chastise all the single men in the church for letting her get away. They are passing up one of the brightest stars of glory in the eternities. Her beauty there will shine for all to see, leaving the spiritually inept 'Cover Girls' looking rather bland.

"Thanks, Jill," I said sincerely. "I'm so glad you're here."

"Yeah," she said, blowing her nose into a tear-stained tissue. "Now I know why I made the reservations for ten days instead of three."

"You know, there are many coincidences like that," I said. "I saw a blue trike at the store yesterday which was identical to Jordy's red trike. I thought of how perfect it would be; the twins could each have one when they grow up, and meanwhile Jordy would have one of each color without wearing either of them out so they'd be in good shape for Ben and Matthew. I wanted to buy it now, because they change models so fast these days I might not find one later. I had the money; it was even on sale, but for some reason I didn't buy it. Why? That's not like me."

"That's for sure, "Jill said, cheering up somewhat. "You never miss a sale."

"Be nice," I said. "I'm not that bad, am I?"

The doorbell chimed, and Jill mouthed a big, "Yes" as she stood to answer it.

Sheri Skiba was at the door. She'd come to take me back to Good Samaritan, where I would stay with Matthew for the next day or two.

Sheri had helped to organize the baby's shower.

"I don't know if you want to return these or not...." She said, handing me the store receipt for their car seats.

Neither did I. Thinking about all the things I would be returning brought more tears. It hurt too much to even imagine.

At the hospital, Sheri showed me how the apnea monitor worked, and what to do when it went off. Most of the time she said it would be false alarms, and she was right. It was so important for me to hear advice from an expert I knew personally. I marveled at

Sister Browne's "prompting" to call Sheri as my Visiting Teacher. Nobody in the ward knew as much about the hospital, CPR, or a heart and lung monitor than Sheri Skiba.

I thanked her for all of her help, and watched as she leaned over the cold steel crib to kiss Matthew goodnight.

He seemed to be content, and oblivious to the wires attached to his chest. He didn't seem to miss Benjamin. I didn't know if that made me feel sad or relieved. Mostly I felt numb.

As I sat beside him on my own little cot, I remembered something strange.

Most of the women at the baby shower brought cute little outfits for the boys along with donating toward the car seats. Of the seventeen sets of clothes the twins had received, no two were the same, and they were in all different sizes. Matthew would be the best-dressed child in town for the next two years, and I wouldn't be faced with the difficult task of returning *any* of the outfits.

It was almost as if each woman had been prompted *not* to buy identical clothing. Another woman in the 24th Ward had twin boys shortly after mine were born. Nearly every outfit she received was in a newborn size, two of each, and matching.

I stretched out on my hospital cot and closed my eyes.

Never had I been so tired, or so unable to sleep. I counted every breath Matthew took, and finally, I took him out of the hospital crib. Sleep came only when I snuggled him closely beside me.

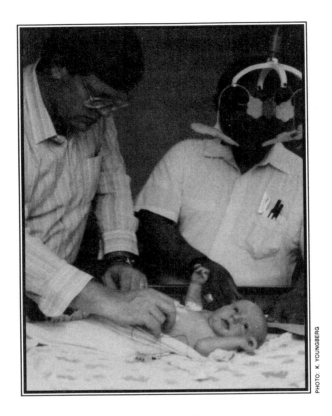

*Eric with Matthew at Good Samaritan
Hospital, learning to use the apnea
monitor. June 16, 1991*

CHAPTER 8

Anger and Peace

Sunday morning was the low point of my life. I truly wanted to die. All the words of all the medical professionals, social workers, and S.I.D.S. Experts meant nothing. I felt as if I was dead myself, and that I had gone to the wrong place. I was a small, cold, heavy lump of coal. I curled up into a fetal position and cried as I remember crying when I was a child about Rachel's age, and found my pet rabbit had died.

At that time in my young life, my rabbit was everything. I cried all that day. I remember sitting in my yellow bathtub that evening with Jill hollering at me to "be quiet!" My mother ranted, *"Nobody could be that sad,"* and my father came home from work and asked, "Has she been crying like that all day?"

This pain was much worse. I wanted more than anything to join Benjamin in his little coffin. I felt there would be plenty of room in its 22 inch length for both of us.

The RN on duty dropped everything she was doing to hold me.

She rocked me as if I were a little baby myself. She had me concentrate on her eyes, and breathe slowly, as I had done with Eric when I was in heavy labor, to get past the pain. She told me that my other children needed me and that Eric needed me, but what got me through was my little Matthew. He cried to be nursed, and I knew he needed me.

I kept apologizing to the nurse for taking her time away from patients, but she said I, too, was a patient.

After I'd nursed Matthew and was alone again, I lay down on my little cot beside the steel crib. I was amazed at what a good nurser Matthew had suddenly become. Until now, he had always preferred a bottle. He nursed so well, I never felt the discomfort of having too much milk. It was as if he had been waiting for Benjamin to die before taking his turn at my breast.

All at once I felt a peace come over me, and I felt the power of prayers directed toward me. In my mind, I could see Julia Hatch. She was the artist, and someone I'd not call an actual friend, though I might wish it. She had tears in her eyes, and I heard her earnestly praying for my family and me. The feeling was so intense I looked at the clock so I could tell Eric about it when he returned. It was 8:47 Sunday morning.

It was Father's Day.

I had enjoyed the best Mother's Day of my life-all five of my children presenting me with breakfast in bed. How Eric managed to make it and deliver it-cold toast and all-I'll never know. All seven of us sat on our bed as I ate it.

Now it was his day; his turn to celebrate and relish his fatherhood...it didn't seem fair. I wished I could give him the day I had enjoyed.

Eric sat through Father's Day at church the day after Benjamin died. He said it never occurred to him *not* to attend church. He wasn't sick. He heard all the talks about fatherhood; children; new babies; love.

He arrived late, which is easy to do when your ward meets at 8:30 in the morning. He missed the announcements, when Bishop Kusch informed the ward of Benjamin's death, and told them his funeral would be held on Tuesday.

Habit seemed to take over for Eric, and he went to his church meetings and performed his duties as usual.

Jill stayed home with the children, and noticed how differently each handled the situation.

Rachel wanted to call all of her friends and talk to them in great detail. In fact, she had called one friend as the paramedics raced out the door. Eric, unable to be understanding at that moment, angrily said, "Don't call anyone!" It was several hours before anyone realized that Rachel really needed to talk to her friends, and felt that she had been permanently forbidden from telling them about her brother's death. Once she had talked it over with everyone, she felt much better and became her usual cheerful self quite rapidly.

David internalized much of his pain. He spent time alone in his room, mostly in bed, and never changed from his pajamas the day Ben died. He has always had difficulty admitting his angry feelings, and he required a great deal of our time and love over a much longer period. He needed to be told over and over that it was okay to cry—that he could be angry—that it really wasn't fair that he lost his baby brother. His understanding of the gospel seemed at times to make it more difficult for him to get past Benjamin's death. David knew that it was part of God's plan. He understood that completely. What he couldn't deal with were his own feelings of anger, which he considered wrong, for not being able to graciously accept the Lord's will.

Eric spent long hours with David, helping him to see that anger is a necessary part of life and death while we live here on earth. Using the Scriptures, Eric taught him how Jesus showed anger when he cleared the temple of the money changers, of the challenges faced by Alma, and how anger helped move the Nephites to action when the warring Lamanites threatened the lives of their wives and children.

"Anger is necessary," Eric explained, "in order for you to understand and fully appreciate peace."

"But if Heavenly Father's plan means that Benjamin has to go back to live with him, I should feel happy, not sad or angry." David said.

"Why should Heavenly Father get him?" Eric countered. "He was *your* brother."

"Yeah." David said, looking at his feet, but not reacting.

It was several days after the funeral before David was finally able to let go and become angry. When he did, it was manifested in a very physical way, with lots of thrashing about, throwing things, and punching his bed and pillow. He said he could have saved him if he'd just gotten him out of his crib instead of staying in bed reading his "Where's Waldo" book that morning. He'd overheard a paramedic say Benjamin had stopped breathing only a few minutes before the ambulance arrived. "I was awake," he sobbed, "I should have saved him."

I was able to hold him and comfort him and cry with him. I told him again how, with S.I.D.S., nobody could have saved him.

Even as I reassured David, I knew I still felt that somehow I, too, should have been able to save him. I *knew* he was going to die. All my life I'd had dreams, visions, and divine manifestations.

When Jill and I were children, we played with a baby boy paper doll. We didn't like sharing much, so we traced him and all of his clothes, making 'twin boys'. We played with them nearly every day, and once, after a death in the family, we played 'funeral' and buried the paper doll baby we'd cloned. I don't know what a psychiatrist would make of that, but I feel it was in some small way a preparation.

After the paper dolls were finally worn out, (you can only tape the legs back on about seventeen times before they're useless) Jill and I got twin baby boy dolls for Christmas. They were larger than life-size, and each had his own little square, wooden playpen. They wore "real" (size 2!) baby clothes, and we loved dressing them alike and floating them in our cement wading pool in the summer. We never played that *they* died, but I remember throwing my twin off our bunkbed a time or two. (I was heavily into 'Superman' at the time.) I forget what my doll was named, but Jill still has her "Jon-Jon".

Were these mere coincidences? I don't think I believe in coincidences anymore. Everything, small or grand, is preparatory in some way for what our purpose is on earth.

So what was the plan? Even as I tried to stop David from blaming himself, I couldn't stop myself from blaming me! How could I have missed these warnings? I'd known since I could remember that I would have twins, and that one of them would die. I had even shared these fears with others; some even years before I was ever married or pregnant.

Despite my advanced warnings, I slept as he died. Were these warnings to prepare me for his inevitable death, or to enable me to prevent it?

Thoughts like these made me crazy. I tried not to think of them; they hurt too deeply.

In the days before the funeral it was good for everyone to have something important to do.

We pressed the missionaries into service. Eric wrote a note thanking our friends and neighbors for the help they'd been to us. It included a detailed map with the time and place of Benjamin's funeral and directions to the chapel. Our ward missionaries passed the notes to our neighbors and others we indicated, including our physicians and our children's teachers.

Eric stopped by work after hours to drop off a note to his secretary informing his co-workers of our plans. I knew this news would be hard for everyone in Eric's working circle. They had all gone out of their way to see our twins. Eric's boss had even come to the hospital when they were only a day old.

At the baby shower thrown for us at the Santa Clara Hewlett-Packard site, I remembered how Benjamin had been passed from person to person. As we were leaving, I collected the babies, putting Matthew and Jordy into the double-stroller. One woman still held Benjamin, and she was dancing around the decorated conference room, showing him off to everyone like a proud grandparent.

"Oh, no," she teased, "I'm keeping Benjamin. You already have two in there, you don't need Ben." He seemed to have that effect on everyone who saw him.

Hewlett-Packard was wonderful to us. After Benjamin's death we received a personal note from John Young, who was then the company president. Eric's immediate boss let him know that he could take paid personal time off for as long as he needed it. That lifted such a burden from Eric's shoulders he was able to be the strong leader we all needed.

Former Bishop Alden Harper and his wife, Marge, stopped by one day before the funeral. They came in the late afternoon without calling first. We were so happy to see them, and invited them to come in and sit down.

Most people seemed to think we needed to be alone in our grief. We really *needed* others to grieve with us, or at least show us they were still in town.

Bishop Harper seemed to know that what I needed more than anything else was to know that Ben's life meant something to someone besides me. I desperately wanted him to be remembered.

Bishop Harper had written this poem:

BABY BENJAMIN

Oh, what a spirit he must have been
not to have mortal trials and sin.
Such are blessed and very rare
and his passing is so hard to bear.
You need not worry nor ever fret
for where he is he is better yet.

He has passed on, your Benjamin,
and one day you will see him again.
The Lord's ways are higher than ours
just as the earth is beneath the stars.
Although short was his mortal stay,
the Lord has for him a better way.
His mortal life is a stepping stone
to a better life the Lord has shown.
Your son has achieved his mission here,
of course, you miss him and shed a tear.
Be consoled in this one important fact;
that we are judged by how we act.
Little children are innocent and pure;
he is with the Lord, of this I am sure.

By C. Alden Harper June 16, 1991

The Harper's came to visit without an official calling or reason to come. We will always be thankful to them for caring about us. We asked Bishop Harper to read his poem at Benjamin's funeral.

Our family in Holland
Rachel, 4 and David, 6. April, 1987

C H A P T E R 9

Gifts of the Spirit

My mother always said I had the unusual spiritual gift of knowing about things before they happened. Besides the extraordinary ability of knowing when the telephone would ring, who was calling and what they wanted, I often knew her secret thoughts and feelings, and would occasionally answer a question before it was asked. This was usually misunderstood, particularly in school.

This gift has always been part of my life, and often I have wondered why I would be given such a divine blessing. It is also a frustration, as it cannot be turned on and off at my own bidding, but is manifest only when the Lord sees fit.

One thought I have had as to it's purpose, is that I have not had an easy life. Besides numerous medical problems, I am Dyslexic, and the majority of the world is not. I see things differently, and have had trouble being comfortable in many classroom and social situations. Dyslexics are usually intuitive. Maybe that is where I got it. I'm in good company; Thomas Edison, Walt Disney, and Albert Einstein were Dyslexic. According to one expert, the founder of our church, Joseph Smith, Jr.,was also Dyslexic.

My growing up years were also complicated by living with a good LDS mother and a father who was faultless unless he was drunk, which was several times per week. He was emotionally and occasionally physically abusive toward us. As the oldest, I felt responsible for everything that went wrong, and I could not hold my tongue against my father. My sister, Jill, was the peacemaker. The younger children suffered most, as Dad's alcoholism grew worse. By that time I had left home to escape his wrath.

Once, in a drunken stupor, my father said he planned to kill the entire family, one at a time, by breaking our necks. He said he would kill me last, so I would be forced to watch everyone else die. He said he had planted C-2 all over the house and yard, and would blow us all "to kingdom come" to destroy the evidence. I had no idea what C-2 was, but since my father had been a Marine Corps Raider who survived Guadalcanal, Iwo Jima, and Pearl Harbor, I had no doubt he knew what he was doing, and would kill us. I called the police many times. They came and said they were sorry, but they couldn't do anything until he carried out a threat. In fear of our own lives being lost, I tried to enlist Jill's aid in killing our father before he could kill us. Fortunately, she kept her wits about her, and we prayed for God to find an answer. He did.

Early one morning at about 2:30, I was awake, kneeling on the middle of my bed when the phone rang. Families of alcoholics often wake at 2:30 a.m. because the bars close at two, and we start praying then. We pray for many things. We pray that he won't crash and kill anyone else. We pray that he will crash and kill himself. It's an insane mixture of relief and anger once he manages to get the car and himself home in one piece.

When the phone rang, I knew instantly that it was the hospital, and that my father was near death. I pulled my jeans on and was nearly dressed when my mom came to tell me what I already knew. Dad was in intensive care for two months. He'd been pronounced "Dead on Arrival" at the hospital, but a man at the morgue recognized my father. He'd served with him in the Korean Conflict.

"That's Andy," he said. "He ain't dead. Ain't nothin' can kill Andy."

He wheeled my father's body back into the emergency room, where he was revived.

It took many more trials, and several more years, but Jill was right. My father repented and became the father and husband he needed to be for us. I am sick with self-loathing whenever I recall the plans I nearly carried out to end his life. I was thinking only of our suffering. I would have destroyed his ability to repent in the flesh, and sealed my own damnation.

Everyone is given different spiritual gifts. My daughter's gift is a beautiful singing voice, and my oldest son was given an inventive mind. We can't "trade" if we admire another's gift more than our own. I'm learning to accept my gift, and try to determine what good I can do with it.

One thing I know I can't do is receive revelation for anyone but my own family. Once I thought I had, and I told a perfect stranger many things I thought my gift had uncovered for her to know. I caused her a great deal of pain, and I'm still repenting for listening to the wrong spirit.

Listening to the right spirit has enlightened my life.

As I young girl, I vividly remember saying good-bye to my grandparents one day in late September. My grandmother, Margret Hobson Sorensen, was standing on her front porch with Elick Joseph Sorensen, my grandfather. The sun was beginning to set, and long, golden rays of sunlight reflected off her taffeta dress with the big purple-blue tulips on it.

"*Take a long look,*" I heard the spirit whisper, "*for this is the last time you will see your grandmother in this life.*"

Our station wagon was already rolling, and I cried and screamed at my mother to turn back. After two blocks, she returned, but not to placate me. She had forgotten her shower cap. (A necessity in the days of beehive hair-do's, which she wore.) I used the moment to tell my grandmother how much I loved her, and to kiss and hug her one last time.

When she died, two months later, I was sad, but I knew Heavenly Father was in control. Though I never saw her again in this life, I was allowed a very personal and profound experience in the Manti Temple many years later which showed me there is only a thin veil separating our two worlds. Sometimes it is thin enough to see through.

A week before Eric and I were married in the Oakland Temple, my parents were sealed in the Manti Temple. Jill and I were there to be sealed to them. We hoped someday our other sister and brothers would desire the blessings of the temple. Jill had recently completed her mission, and was allowed to attend my parents sealing. I waited in the beautiful and recently restored Celestial Room of the Manti Temple until I would be called in to be sealed to my parents.

As I waited, I thought over many spiritual experiences, and felt a blessed peace all around and through me. In that most sacred of places on earth, I pondered these things, and prayed to be the kind of wife Eric deserved.

"How does it feel to be on the outside?"

I turned, but nobody was there. At least no one my natural eyes could view.

"How does it feel to be on the outside?"

The question came again to my soul; I knew instantly that my grandfather, E. J. Sorensen, stood beside me in the Celestial Room.

"Remember this feeling," he said. *"Trust in Our Lord Jesus Christ, and endure to the end."*

I felt his presence pass in front of me, and as he did, I saw a distortion in the mirror directly across from me. It took my breath away as I realized I had actually seen the manifestation of a spirit.

My surprise was not over, for after he passed, another, smaller form, followed him. I knew that my grandmother, Margret, was beside him. The mirror outlined her spirit like heat-waves rising from a desert mirage. I knew absolutely that they were there, and if I remained worthy, I could be with them some day.

I watched what I could feel more than see, as they stood before the door of my parents sealing room. My grandfather raised his hand, as if to knock, and turned once again to me. *"Remember this feeling,"* he said. *"You want to be on the inside at the last day. Endure to the end."* They then passed quietly into the sealing room through the closed door.

After the sealing, my mother embraced me, and with tears flowing, said, "There were two empty chairs in the back of the room, did you see them?"

"I saw them", I said, "but they weren't empty."

"I know!" my mother said, crying softly. "My mother and father were here."

As long as I was worthy, the Holy Ghost was a constant companion. When David was only a few weeks old, I put him down to nap. I knew he would sleep for at least two hours, giving me time to sew him some flannel night shirts.

After only a few seams, I heard the Spirit whisper, *"Run,"* and I did.

David was batting his arms and legs in a frenzy. His face was screwed up into an intense howl, but not a sound escaped his lips, which were quite blue.

I vaulted over the couch and scooped him up and over my head in one fluid movement.

My thumbs compressed his tiny diaphragm, and he sputtered and choked, coughing out a wad of white paper which proved to be a straw wrapper from the hospital. I don't know how he got it, but I collapsed to my knees, thanking God for getting it out. Then I had no knowledge of the Heimlich Maneuver, and if left to my own sensibilities, would most likely have hit him on the back, lodging it further.

Two years later my garage was being used as a polling place for the November election. As I chatted with my neighbors, I was suddenly interrupted by the Holy Ghost. I don't recall any words this time, only an intense feeling to check on Rachel, who was then six weeks old.

I ran to her crib. She had stopped breathing.

I screamed for Loretta Schader, my neighbor and Visiting Teaching companion who was in my garage helping with the election.

She ran down the hall as I grabbed Rachel and yelled at Loretta to call 9-1-1.

Rachel began breathing on her own, and never had another episode. She was blessed indeed, because this indicates the possibility of sleep apnea, which can cause death. She should have been monitored, but not knowing this, I didn't worry, and never gave it another thought. In fact, I forgot entirely about the episode until Loretta asked me after Ben's death if there could have been a connection.

Most of Rachel's early life I have forgotten. Her birth had disturbed the critical hormonal balance in my body, and I suffered greatly with post-partum depression. Undiagnosed, my depression continued nearly five years.

Every doctor I visited would ask me if I was depressed. I always said "no." How could I possibly be depressed? I had a wonderful family, a husband I adored, and the gospel of Jesus Christ in my life. We were living in Scotland and later in The Netherlands, making trips to Sweden, Israel, France, Africa, and a dozen other countries just for fun. We had no financial worries, and were emotionally close to our extended families. It was ridiculous to suggest I could be depressed.

Yet I was, and about a year after we returned to the states, I was finally diagnosed and helped with anti-depressant drugs.

Taking a medication went against everything I'd come to believe about being in charge of my own life and feelings. I now admit that

I was wrong. It is very wrong to think you can "pull yourself up by your own bootstraps" or "snap out of it" if your problem is mental. The mind is controlled by the brain, which is part of the body, and is often upset as easily as the stomach can become upset. Sometimes the solution can be as simple as an antacid for the stomach. In my case, this was true. After only two months of medication, I was my old self again. However, I was angry that my condition had taken so long to diagnose. It was as if I'd lost five years of my life. I wished a doctor had asked, "Do you feel sad without a reason to feel sad? Did this happen all at once? When did it happen?" So many doctor's were so quick to say, "It's PMS; we can't do anything to help you."

We also discovered that during a surgery I had on my jaw (TMJ) shortly after Rachel's birth I was given Teflon implants which have since been recalled. Tests indicate that the implants dissolved and may have been absorbed into my system, which could be the reason for my immune system problems, as well as the depression. Being in constant physical pain from all of these medical difficulties can cause mental stress as well.

These experiences have helped me to feel much more empathy for others suffering physical and mental illnesses. They really can happen to anyone.

Though I still face more surgery, I recovered emotionally, and Eric felt the girl he'd married had been returned. The difference was incredible to me. Life was fun again. I took delight in every experience. I stopped being tired all day, and I was able to stop the medication after only eight weeks of treatment.

Right away I wanted to have another baby. This came as quite a shock to Eric, who remembered the teary woman who had told him years before that two children were all she could handle.

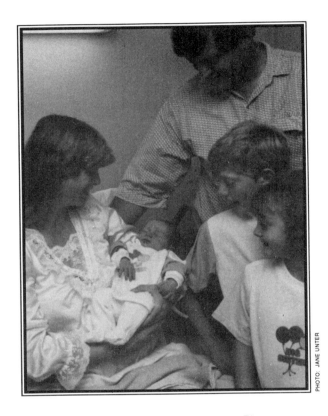

August 23, 1989—David, 9, Rachel, 7
Jordy is just a few hours old

CHAPTER 10

Memories and Miracles

Matthew slept most of the time at the hospital, but I needed to stay there beside him for my own peace of mind. It was good to have three days to myself to sort memories before the funeral. It seemed I had total recall of every minute of Benjamin's short life.

One night in particular I remember Eric and I being up non-stop. It was very late, and neither of us had gotten any sleep.

Eric tended to Matthew's needs, and I tried to get Benjamin settled. Nothing worked. At one point I was walking him in the hall. I held him at eye-level, yelling at him to stop crying and go to sleep. I think I would have shaken him if I hadn't been taught about the dangers involved in shaking a baby, which I was very careful never to do. We stood there, eye to eye, and communicated.

Some may call it my tired and over-active imagination. Others may say it was 'the still, small voice'. I happen to know that Benjamin spoke to me. I know, because I'd heard him speak to me before.

I recognized his spirit talking to mine.

"Don't be angry with me, Mother," he said. *"If you are, you will always remember, and you will never forgive yourself."*

I didn't care how tired I was after that. I took Benjamin to my rocking chair, and for forty-five minutes, I loved him tenderly. I sang to him. I stroked his face, absorbing every millimeter of it. I told him stories of our family, of fun times we had enjoyed together, of our traditions and of my love for him.

How I treasure that memory! How thankful I am for it! How I would have suffered had I become angry, or possibly done something to hurt him.

Eric was suffering.

"I feel like it's my fault," he explained. "Because of what I said that night...don't you remember what I said? I can't forget it. I held one of the babies in the air, over my head, and yelled at God, *'One baby would have been plenty!'"*

I couldn't recall the event until after he told me, and then I did remember, but I laughed and hugged him hard. I assured him that *I* knew what he meant, and I knew our Heavenly Father did, too. Ben's death was not anyone's fault. It was part of a plan.

So why did Benjamin die? Why was he born? What is the 'master plan' set up by The Master of us all?

Spencer W. Kimball, twelfth president of the church, said in his talk, *Tragedy or Destiny?,*

"I am positive in my mind that the Lord has planned our destiny. Sometime we'll understand fully, and when we see back from the vantage point of the future, we shall be satisfied with many of the happenings of this life that are so difficult to comprehend." (p.11)

The first time I was pregnant, I also carried twins. I miscarried at church when we were first living in the valley, in the San Jose 6th Ward.

A woman in the ward helped me. She was very upset, and crying that I had lost the baby. I had held the small embryo in my hand,

and felt a reassuring calm settle upon me. Spirit spoke to spirit. *"If thou wilt,"* he whispered, *"I will return."*

At the hospital, a miracle happened. The emergency room physician had worked a double shift and was exhausted. He asked a few questions, and without even examining me, ordered me to bed without the usual D & C procedure to cleanse my uterus. Had that occurred, David would not have been born, full-term and healthy, (8 pounds, 14 ounces) on September second, seven months later.

Miscarriage of one fraternal twin was deemed "possible, but remote" in 1980. Now the medical community has determined that many more twins are conceived than are born, and that the loss of a twin in utero is not as uncommon as was once thought. Widespread use of ultrasound imaging systems has helped to bring this phenomenon to light.

During the five years of my depression after Rachel's birth, I did everything I could to try to convince myself that the "spirit voice" I had heard after my miscarriage of David's twin, was Rachel's. I was ill. I couldn't handle more children. I tried not to think about it, yet I knew Rachel was not that spirit. That spirit was male.

One day, before I became pregnant with Jordan, I was having an especially good communion with my Father in Heaven. I was struck with His goodness and love for me, and I knew that He had forgiven me of my numerous sins, so grievous to me. As I cried my thankfulness to Him, I asked Him sincerely if there was anything I could do for Him.

I remained on my knees several minutes, then stood up and prepared for the morning' activities.

Light particle like suspended rain began to fill the room. I was not at all frightened, or even curious, as I am about almost everything around me. Instead, I was completely calm. I felt the presence of someone in the light, and I knew he was a messenger from behind the veil.

A sound I can't describe in words came to me, and a strong,

masculine voice, quiet, almost whispering, very plainly said;

"A valiant spirit body needs to be born...."

Though it was stated, I knew it to be a question I had to answer.

"I will bear him," I volunteered without hesitation, but realized an instant later the full implication of such a birth. Valiant Spirits are usually those who need a body only to fulfill the covenant of the flesh. Valiant Spirits die young. I thought of taking back my words. Did I have the strength to lose a child without losing my faith? What about Eric? David and Rachel? Our family?

"Because of your faith, you will be blessed."

As the light gathered and departed, the messenger left with it, and as he left, I knew somehow that I had been promised twins, and that one of them would die.

I called Eric home from work to tell him about the experience. He never questioned the reality of the messenger, but he was skeptical of my sudden change-of-heart. Since he had always hoped for more children, he was more than willing to try again. I couldn't wait to get pregnant.

During the pregnancy, I told my doctor all about the twins I was carrying. I knew one of them was male, but I hoped for a female, too. He humored me, as I had the entire family there to watch the ultrasound of my twins. To represent my babies, I even put pom-poms on my belly; pink for the girl, and a blue one for the boy. The ultrasound confirmed only one male child. Jordan. The kids were disappointed not to see twins, but Eric and I were downright scared. Would this baby die?

Eric sat up late many nights with me as I cried my fears. I was afraid Jordan was the Valiant Spirit. Whenever we talked to David and Rachel about the baby I carried, we stressed, "not all babies live." We had Family Home Evening lessons about the purpose of life, and what happens when we die. We felt we prepared them as much as we could for the possibility of the baby's death.

Though we knew he would be a boy, we wouldn't allow ourselves or the children to call him by name. Once Eric became uneasy when Rachel said, "Hi, Jordan," to my enlarged belly. "Until he's born," Eric informed her, "he hasn't got a name."

Jordan was blessed without problems of any kind. During his birth, I experienced one of my most memorable and beautiful visions into the veil.

Most women who bear children notice that each birth becomes physically easier. In my case, each became more difficult. Jordan's birth was especially painful, and at one point, I prayed for "a small glimpse" of him, to feel more connected to him; more able to draw upon all my power to push him out.

In my mind, I suddenly saw a small, very distinctive square ear. I knew it was Jordan's ear, and as I prayed my thanks and continued the birth, I realized we were in trouble. I could not deliver him without medical intervention.

Dr. Smith, my obstetrician, ordered an emergency room prepared, and my friend Jane rushed David and Rachel from the delivery room to the waiting area.

Eric was able to accompany me into the emergency delivery room, where Dr. Smith prepared a vacuum device with which to extract Jordan.

Eric and I had recently seen the film, *Spartacus*. Toward the end of the film is a scene where a huge battle takes place. Hills are virtually covered with the warring armies. A similar scene unfolded above me in the delivery room.

Hills stretching as far as I could see were covered with people clothed in white. Thousands, perhaps even a million people were thus assembled. All were watching me, and I understood them to be part of my eternal family. I was related in some way to each of those people. It amazed me. As I continued to watch, two people broke away from the top of the throng, and the multitude divided, making a path for the two men, who were walking toward me.

As they came closer, I recognized the one on the right to be

Eric's father, who had passed away six months after our marriage. He looked younger and stronger, but it was definitely Leland.

The man beside him seemed familiar, but I didn't know him. As they came closer, I realized the man was becoming shorter; smaller; younger. He was a young man, then a boy, then a toddler, and Leland bent down and scooped him up, smiling as he came closer to me.

The toddler became a smaller baby, and, as they reached me, a newborn infant.

Leland broke out in a smile I can only describe as that of a very proud and happy grandpa. It was a smile I'd never seen him give in life, but I saw it now—broad and beautiful—as he handed the baby to me, and I heard Jordan's first cry.

Later that day, as Jordan slept at my side in his isolette at the hospital, I remembered the little ear I had seen in my vision. I struggled to sit up to see his distinctive square ear.

A tiny, newborn ear, round as can be, enhanced his cherubic face. *"Oh, well..."* I thought. *"It served its purpose at the time."*

I slept peacefully that night.

The next day as I was observing the miracle of each tiny toe and finger, I suddenly screamed out loud.

A nurse who was changing the bed next to mine was alarmed and asked me what on earth was the matter.

"His ear!" I screamed. "I was looking at his left side yesterday! It's round, but this is *his* ear; the one I saw before he was born! His sweet little square ear! It's right here on the other side! I never thought to turn him over to check the right side!"

The nurse must have thought I was crazy, but she humored me, telling me his ear was perfectly normal. "Lot's of babies have funny ears when they are born, but they straighten out later," she said. I didn't care how it looked later. I thanked my Heavenly Father for his care and blessing, and snuggled my beautiful new baby boy. I knew he would stay and become part of our family. When I thought about the "Valiant Spirit" I consoled myself by saying, "it must have been a test". Deep inside, I knew it wasn't over, but I rejoiced at having my beautiful Jordan, so precious and dear.

Slipping into the past was easier than facing the present. I wished my spiritual gift would tell me what to do next. Tomorrow was Benjamin's funeral.

Jubillation! We're expecting twins!
December, 1990

C H A P T E R   1 1

Faith Without Fear

Matthew was released from the hospital Monday night. We took him home to anxious siblings, relieved to have him back.

The apnea monitor sounded many times that night. I found myself with a lot of time to think as I rocked Matthew in the same rocking chair I had used to soothe all of my children.

I thought back to that December day when I was going in for an amniocentesis test. This test involves insertion of a long needle into the amniotic sac to withdraw fluid that can be analyzed to determine many types of birth defects and genetic abnormalities, as well as determining for certain the sex of the child. I'd had one during my pregnancy with Jordan due to medical conditions that run in my family. Never would I terminate a pregnancy if I found the condition present, but I felt knowing what to expect in advance could help me to better deal with a problem emotionally, and prepare a medical team at the delivery to be available from the start of his life.

The joy of Jordan's successful birth or perhaps the veil being drawn again had caused me to forget the encounter with the Heavenly Messenger regarding the Valiant Spirit whom I had agreed to bear.

As I conferred with the genetic counselor prior to the amniocentesis, I was amazed at how fast she documented my own little "family tree" with symbols for my children, male and female. David's miscarried fraternal twin was even included, which pleased me immensely. She used the symbol for a male, which I found quite remarkable. I asked her why she chose to make him a male, since we didn't know the sex.

"Funny you should ask..." she said. "In embryo, we are all female, and I usually denote that on miscarriages occurring in the first trimester. I don't really know...I just felt he was male. Did you have any particular feelings as to the sex? Shall I record a female symbol?"

"No, no," I said, smiling. "I know you are right. I just wondered how you knew he was a male."

I was feeling at the peak of my health and very contented with life.

"Boy, girl, boy...this one has to be a girl." I thought to myself. *"Heavenly Father has certainly spoiled me; I always get everything I want."*

Nearly skipping into the amniocentesis room, I hopped up onto the table and waited for the technician.

When he arrived, he applied the jelly to my bulging tummy and hooked up the wires. He looked at his monitor. He wouldn't let me see it, and told me to just lie still and he'd show me after he took the measurements.

In a silly mood, I told him if he found a boy in there, to please change him into a girl.

He didn't laugh.

"Is this your first baby?" He chirped like an overworked diplomat, forced to act cheerfully.

"No," I answered, grinning like a chimpanzee. "It's my fourth."

He promptly excused himself from the room.

"Probably throwing up," I reasoned. Californian's in this area rarely have more than one child. Two tops. Three kids and people think you are threatening the ecological balance of the planet.

When he came back, another man, a doctor, was with him.

"Uh-oh," I thought.

Suddenly I was surrounded by white light. If you've ever seen the movie, *GHOST,* where Patrick Swayze is taken up into heaven at the end, that's what this light was like, only not so obvious. (I later saw *GHOST* and got goose bumps remembering this experience.)

It was as if the light was holding me up. I was weightless. The men in the room didn't seem to notice anything unusual, but I was wide-eyed, wondering what was going on, yet not at all frightened.

"Hold on" the wordless thoughts came into my mind. *"You are in for the roller-coaster ride of your life. Faith. Have Faith."*

There was a lot more about faith, which was the prevailing message, but it zoomed by me like the fast-forward on a VCR. I can't really say what it said, because I don't think it came in actual words; it was more like feelings, which I understood as a whole.

Then, as quickly as it came, it was gone. The medical men were turning the monitor around to show me.

The technician made a big deal out of saying, "Here is your baby" and on and on about his head and feet, and then saying, "and here is your other baby," as if I couldn't tell they were twins the instant he turned the screen around.

"Are you sure there are only two in there?" I teased.

Though I could see only two, I suddenly remembered an old Chinese photographer who had taken a family portrait of us just two months before.

"You carry triplets," he had stated matter-of-factly.

Eric and I exchanged surprised glances, as my pregnancy was not yet apparent, and we had not mentioned to him that I was expecting. I wondered what kind of camera he was using...X-ray?

"I take free family photo if you come back next year with triplets," he said.

I smiled, wondering if twins would count.

"I think I deserve triplets," I said to the technician, still giddy from the news of twins.

The men were busy with the needles necessary for the amniocentesis, and ignored my little jokes.

They began to explain the procedure, how two needles must be used because of the two separate amniotic sacs, and how purple dye must be injected into the first to ensure that they wouldn't examine the same sac twice.

"Since they are twins," I heard myself say, "I'd prefer not to proceed with the amniocentesis."

It was a prompting from the Holy Ghost, and I knew He was right. I feared the men would be angry, since I had the appointment scheduled weeks in advance, and they had already prepared the first injection. Instead, they both seemed relieved. The technician exhaled, as if he'd been holding his breath.

"Is there more danger involved with twins?" I asked. I seemed to sense that one could kick the other at the wrong moment, but I really didn't know. I was curious, because my sudden change of heart was based purely on instinct. That, and a fairly strong suggestion from behind the veil.

"Technically, no," said the doctor, "But with a multiple pregnancy, nothing can be assumed."

I remember shaking when I got into the car to drive myself home. It was kind-of like I'd felt as a child after eating an entire bag of Trick-or-Treats.

"Great," I thought. *"Eric is on the East Coast, touring nuclear submarines! He'll be out of town for two whole weeks-this is not the kind of message I can spring on him over the phone."*

Clutching the ultrasound photograph in my hand, I tried to drive without looking at it every three seconds.

"Eric is going to love hearing that the van needs a thousand dollar transmission job, both older kids need braces, and now we'll really need that bigger home. May as well save it all up and hit him with everything at once as soon as he gets home," I thought, smiling to myself as I imagined the critical moment.

Since I couldn't tell Eric for two weeks, I had to tell someone close to me. Instead of going home, I headed for Ann's house.

Ann is my cousin, the oldest daughter of my mother's sister. She and her family were living in San Jose after several years abroad, living in Singapore, France, and England. I was her children's nanny in France when her twin girls were born.

She is a few years older than I, and her life seemed to be charting a course mine was destined to follow.

I drove straight to Ann's house and told her I needed a hug.

"I could understand when both of our husband's served missions in Brazil," I said. "I could handle the fact that they both worked for Hewlett-Packard. I was thrilled when both of our families ended up living abroad...but now we'll both have *five* children. You've given me your 'tail end' twins!"

"Oh, Kjirstin," she moaned. "One never jokes about twins."

I showed her the ultrasound photograph, and she oooh'd and aaah'd over it with her twins, Janine and Shantal, looking over her shoulder.

"Now," I said, "just leave your aneurysm to yourself!"

Five years before, Ann had an aneurysm, an enlarged blood vessel that burst in her brain. At that time, only ten-percent of people with aneurysms even lived past the first 24 hours. She was now fully recovered except for some short-term memory loss. She attributed her survival to the priesthood blessing she received from her husband and his brothers as they carried her down Provo Canyon during a family reunion. A Scandinavian doctor happened to be in Utah for a medical convention. He was one of only two brain aneurysm specialists in the world. He was there to help save her life.

Another case of the Lord and His will.

Ann went to her bookshelves and selected several books on twins and twin care.

"These are must-reads." she said, "and some of them are out-of-print now, so I'll loan them to you. You'll have plenty to read while you're on bed-rest for a couple of months."

"I don't think I'll be confined to bed," I said. "I feel terrific."

"Oh, right," she said, stifling a giggle as she walked me to the door. "Merry Christmas," Ann called, waving good-bye as I drove toward home.

I continued to glance at the ultrasound photograph of my babies.

"Oh," I thought. *"I should have asked for two photographs, so they could each have one in their baby books."*

That foreboding feeling I knew so well came once more, and as I looked at "Twin B" I knew something was wrong. I knew that I would only need one photograph.

I forced the feeling deep inside, and turned my thoughts to Christmas.

Christmas had always been a big deal for me. I'd start the day after Thanksgiving, and decorate the entire house. Eric usually came in whistling, "Deck The Halls" because they were *decked!*

Each year we buy a special, dated ornament. When Eric finished his business trip, I waited until he walked in the front door, and then, video-camera rolling, I let our annual Christmas ornament tell him.

"Hmmmmm," he said, as he twirled the little green pea pod ornament in his hand. "It says, 'two peas in a pod'. What could this mean? Twins? We're having twins? You're kidding...you're not kidding... ahhhhhhh!"

Everyone jumped around in jubilation. I watched this home videotape over and over again. It was the most joyful moment in my life.

"How can I ever have Christmas without my two little peas?" I

wondered. *"Christmas!"* I scolded myself. *"Already I'm worried about Christmas!"*

"Oh, Father," I sobbed, back in real time. *"How can I get through tomorrow?"*

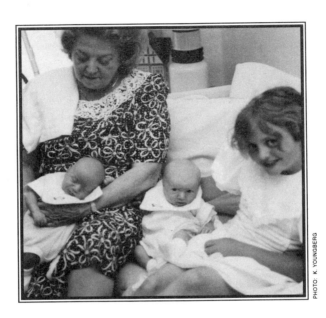

Blessing day, June 2, 1991
Grandma LaRue holds a sleepy
Benjamin, Rachel with Matthew

CHAPTER 12

Changed, Not Destroyed

Benjamin's Funeral Day. A day every parent prays will never come into their life, was in mine. It was nothing like I imagined it. The trepidation I feared, never surfaced. From beginning to end, it was more like my wedding day. A time to share with dear friends and close family members. A time of love so thick I could feel it wrapped around me like my Grandma's down-stuffed quilt.

We awoke to a beautiful spring morning, sunny and warm, like most California days. Standing with my husband in our closet, we reached for the clothes we wore for our twins' blessings. I never considered wearing one of my black dresses or suits, but put on a simple white dress of Thai silk, and a tailored linen jacket.

As I buttoned my dress, my thoughts wandered back to the morning we took our twin sons to church to receive their official names and blessings.

We were going to bless them before my mother had to return to her home in Victorville, but decided to wait until Fast Sunday, when babies were appointed to be named and blessed. Eric's brother, Chris, and his family, would be able to come that day, and Chris could assist in the ordinance.

That morning, however, we realized that neither of us had confirmed with Chris that the blessings would be performed that day, and he didn't come. We decided, thankfully, to bless them anyway.

We sat in the chapel on the rows to the right, close to the front, in full view of everyone as Eric carried Matthew to the podium.

Eric had gone about three steps when I called him back.

"Benjamin is to receive the first blessing," I whispered to him.

"What?" Eric asked, his voice two octaves higher than normal as he tried to whisper without attracting too much attention. All eyes were on him, and I knew there was no time to explain.

I passed Benjamin over to Eric, who whispered, "Matthew was the first-born, remember?"

All I could do was shrug my shoulders and shoot him my best, "Don't-ask-me, I-don't-know-any-more-than-you-do," look. He knew better than to question.

Eric handed Matthew back to me, and took Benjamin to the stand. He asked Bishop Kusch and his counselors to assist in blessing him.

What came forth from Eric's lips in that blessing can only be described as Divine. I had wanted to record the blessings, but had my hands so full of children I was unable to get to my paper and pencil.

Benjamin was promised things I can't even speak, except to say that they were more ethereal than I had ever heard given in any blessing, confirmation, setting apart, or patriarchal blessing. It was more spiritual than a General Conference talk, BYU Devotional, or anything I had ever heard in my life, even in the temple. My breath was taken away, and I felt a strong conviction that Benjamin was choice above all persons I had known or met to that point in my life. This was shocking, as I had walked and talked with world leaders, apostles, and even a future prophet of the church.

His blessing lasted more than ten minutes, and when it was

finished, I could hear people sobbing throughout the chapel.

When Eric handed Benjamin back to me, and took Matthew, he whispered, "I feel weak; what did I say?"

Matthew's blessing was short, and very much like David and Jordan's blessings had been. He was promised a mission and temple marriage if he lived a righteous life.

Later that day, Sister Pat Embley, wife of our former bishop said, "Eric gave beautiful blessings...particularly Benjamin's."

After Benjamin died, Eric and I were in the hospital with Matthew. We counted every breath he took as we watched the lights blink on his monitor. "He's going to be okay," I said. "He doesn't really need this monitor."

"I know," Eric said, "But we're going to use it for as long as the doctor says he needs it."

"Of course," I agreed, "but how can you be so sure he'll be all right. You sound absolutely certain."

Eric was very quiet, but when he finally spoke, I knew it was important for me to remember.

"I know Matthew will survive," he said, "because when I was conferring his blessing upon him, I saw the people he will teach on his mission."

After wiping the tears from my eyes, I faltered, but at last asked Eric what he had seen as he gave Benjamin his name and blessing.

"Nothing," he said. "I saw nothing at all. Nothing but a very bright whiteness."

Reaching back into my closet for my white pumps, I smiled at the memory. We had so much to be thankful for it was impossible to feel cheated. I knew absolutely that Jesus Christ stood at the head of our church, and this church is that original church He began during His sojourn on earth. I knew His church had been restored again in these last few days before His return to sanctify it unto Himself. I felt so very thankful for His truths, taught to the people of old in Jerusalem and to the children of Abraham who were in this

New World at the time of his crucifixion, sent here to carry the seeds of Abraham to all corners of the world, and to testify of Christ in these last days. Truths taught by our prophets today; truths that promise us our babies who die are innocent, and return to Him, not to a burning hell from the imagined sins of their parents.

"Is this dress all right, Mommy?" Rachel asked as she stood shyly beside my bedroom door.

Stepping into my shoes, I peered out of my closet at one of the sweetest sights a mother can view. Rachel, so innocent and pure, stood at the door with pink foam curlers in her soft, blond hair. She was wearing the white dress she wore when Eric confirmed her a member of the church after her baptism.

"Perfect," I said, reaching for a hug. "You picked exactly the right dress."

David stood in the hall, looking tall in his navy wool suit. He stared at his feet.

"Do I look okay?" He asked.

"As handsome as your father," I said, including him in our hug.

"No! no! no!" We heard Jordy wail from the living room. Jill was chasing him with his Sunday pants. "No pants!" He yelled. "It not Sunday today!"

It felt good to laugh.

We gathered for family prayer, and then filed solemnly outside. My throat tightened when we opened the van and I saw the three car seats strapped across the back. For a few seconds we all seemed frozen in our places, and then I said, "Jordy can have Ben's car seat. It matches better. Now he can look out the window."

Without a word, Eric took Jordy's old car seat out, and put it in the "give-away" stack in our garage.

Jill strapped the two little ones into their car seats, and sat down between them.

"Ben only got one ride in his car seat," I thought, trying not to feel resentment.

I hated the new van. We had an older van-conversion with a new transmission that ran fine. It was ugly on the outside, but I always thought that made it less likely to attract car thieves. While I was in the hospital with the twins, Eric bought a brand new, fancy-schmancy Ford Explorer van-conversion. He'd consulted with me first, but I guess I wasn't prepared for the sleek grandeur of a full-sized, extra tall, white van with a built-in ice chest, stereo, color TV and VCR with remote control and Nintendo games. We drove in silence to the chapel.

At the church, we embraced relatives and I busied myself thanking Linda Browne.

My cousin, Denise Wilson, was there with her husband, Bud, and I occupied myself showing him how to operate our video camera. I had not forgiven myself for not having a family photograph, and was now obsessed with getting everything on film.

Benjamin was in his little white box on the lace-covered Relief Society table, but I couldn't look. I must have hugged everyone in the room three times before my mother finally took me by the arm and led me firmly to the table.

The Relief Society sisters had set up a lovely display of the few things that were Benjamin's. On top of the easel was the artwork Julia Hatch had painted—the nursery animals spelling out his name in vibrant colors. Below it was a photograph of Jordy, holding Ben and feeding him a little bottle from the hospital. Bishop Harper's poem was next to that, and Ben's Baby Calendar and Baby Book were open on the table.

I thought back to the day, less than a week before, when I'd caught up on the baby books and calendars. I had cut out samples from the wrapping paper of each gift he and Matthew had received and shared the cards equally among them.

Heather, our nanny-helper, had remarked at how thorough I was to keep up with these things. I had laughed and said that her help made it possible-but at the same time I knew it was unusual for me. David and Rachel still had gaps in their baby books, and I knew Jordy's was even less complete.

As I glanced through Benjamin's calendar, I noticed that I had gotten ahead of myself-pasting the stickers on his monthly birthdays before he had them. Later, checking Matthew's calendar, I discovered I'd not been nearly as efficient. I wondered if perhaps I'd sensed his earthly end was close, and thought somehow I could extend his stay by filling in his calendar birthdates months in advance.

My mother led me to Benjamin's body, and I knew I would have to look at him.

"He isn't here;" I thought, *"it's just his shell."* He looked puffy, and had on lots of make-up. He wasn't like my Baby Ben. His lips were painted pink and had been pushed up into an odd smile. Ben's lips had been darker, and shaped like a rosebud.

My darling son, the real Benjamin, was somewhere else, and very much alive. Words from a long ago science class came into my mind, *"Matter cannot be destroyed, only changed to another form."* Joseph Smith had enlightened us more on the subject, and I knew Benjamin's form was now spiritual. He was tall, and strong, and beautiful. Still, I wanted to embrace his physical body, to kiss him, and let him know some way how very much I loved him.

One by one, the children came up to view Benjamin's body. Rachel wanted to take him out of the casket, and hold him one last time, but we explained that could not be done. Later, at the cemetery, she wanted to see him before the burial, and we allowed her a private good-bye.

A nurse at the hospital had suggested letting each child write or draw something, or give him a small item they found meaningful.

The demands of the past few days had prevented me from writing. I felt sad, but I remembered the night we had together, rocking, and I knew he understood my love without a note in his casket.

David had a calculator watch he'd had since he was very young. It was missing a strap, but I knew it meant the world to him.

"Oh, this is a stupid thing to give him," he cried, tears stinging his pale blue eyes. I assured him it was just right, and that Ben would know how much it meant to him, and know he loved him. He laid it gently beside the pillow, and touched Ben's cheek.

I opened my eyes widely so my tears wouldn't fall.

Rachel carried a tiny gold star. It was a gift from the producer of the San Jose Civic Light Opera for her performance in EVITA. It was the closest thing she had to a trophy. It was her greatest treasure. I helped her pin it to Ben's little white collar.

"What are you giving Ben, Jill?" Rachel asked my sister.

"All her things are in New York, Rachel," I interrupted, stammering with embarrassment. "She didn't plan on this happening."

Later, in the corner of the casket, I saw Jill's silver CTR ring. Choose The Right, its letters proclaimed. Jill, I knew, had always chosen rightly.

Ben, it seemed, had also chosen the right.

Eric holding Benjamin and Matthew
Late May 1991

C H A P T E R   1 3

A Choice Name

I t was time to go into the chapel. We said our private and final good-byes to Benjamin's earthly body, and watched as the lid was placed upon his casket. Eric's three brothers picked it up, though one could easily have handled it alone. Niel and Chris carried the casket, and John followed with the coverlet of tiny yellow roses. We quietly filed into the sacred room where two weeks before we had witnessed Benjamin's blessing.

When we passed the pews on the right, where we were seated together on that blessing day, for an instant I pled with The Father to turn back the clock; to make it be his blessing day again. I promised to do everything right this time. In my sudden panic, I feared I would break down.

Strength from something stronger than myself bid me look to the left. There I saw my mother and Jill sitting, smiling, with my four beautiful, living children.

I was reminded of a line from the 40th Chapter of Alma, verse 8:

"... all is as one day with God, and time only is measured unto men."
God could turn back the clock, but His will was for Ben to be with
Him. What better place for so perfect a child? He would be in good
hands until mine could once again hold him.

Heavenly support from dozens of prayers followed Eric and me
up to the stand. We stood as Eric's brother's bore Benjamin's casket
and flowers to the front of the chapel.

Memories and conversations flooded back vividly. I returned to
that warm Friday night, sitting on the lawn with Jill and the babies.

"How did you decide their names?" Jill had asked, letting
Matthew explore her outstretched fingers.

"I was told what their names were," I answered.

"What do you mean, 'told'?"

"I don't know, exactly," I explained. "I mean, we knew they were
boys, and we wanted Hebrew names, like our other children, but it
was hard to choose. I wanted different initials, you know..."

"So you can scratch them on the bottom of a paper cup and
know who's is who's...just like Mom did, right?" Jill said, laughing.

"Aawww; you caught me."

"It's okay," Jill said. "I've got a lot of Mom in me, too."

"Anyway, one day I was mopping the kitchen floor and something said to me, 'You shall call the first son Matthew, and the second
is named Benjamin. If they are taken by emergency Cesarean,
Benjamin will be the first-born.' "

"How strange!"

"Yeah! I sure thought so; I asked my doctor about it, and he
said, 'That's right. Due to their positioning, Twin 'B' will be the first
out if it's an emergency Cesarean, but in a natural birth or a planned
Cesarean, we'll cut lower and Twin 'A' will be first.'"

"That is almost too weird."

"Since they were so crowded in there, they stayed where they
were, and I knew who was who. I got to talk to them while they were
still inside. It was fun, and I really got to know them well before

they were born...maybe that's where I first got attached to Ben...he was breech, you know, head up, way up high, just to the right of my heart. Maffy was head down and knocking on the door. He couldn't wait to get out. I spent those two months in bed rubbing and singing to Benjamin. I couldn't even reach Matthew!

"How did you chose their middle names?"

"Middle names were easy. We wanted to honor both Grand-fathers, so I walked across my wet kitchen floor to our marking board and wrote down 'Matthew Leland' and 'Benjamin Carl'. At dinner that night I asked everyone what they thought, and they seemed happy. We may not have any living Grandpa's, but on the other side I know they're proud to have these little guys bear their names."

"I didn't really like the name 'Benjamin'." I'd admitted to Jill that evening. "I thought it was a bit long with a last name like 'Youngberg', but that was in December or January, and from the day I wrote their names on the board, that's who they were."

Thinking back on the conversation sent shivers all over me, and I remembered something I'd read a long time ago in Apostle James E. Talmage's book, *Jesus The Christ*.

"...According to man's judgment there may be but little importance attached to names; but in the nomenclature of the Gods every name is a title of power or station. God is righteously zealous of the sanctity of His own name (Exo. 20:7; Lev. 19:12; Deut. 5:11) and of names given by His appointment. In the case of children of promise names have been prescribed before birth; this is true of our Lord Jesus and of the Baptist, John, who was sent to prepare the way for the Christ. Names of persons have been changed by divine direction, when not sufficiently definite as titles denoting the particular service to which the bearers were called, or the special blessings conferred upon them." (p.35)

While I'd not say my children are "Children of Promise", or that they are any more grand or precious than other children, I do know that Eric and I had very little say in the decision of what to name our three youngest sons.

David means "Beloved" and Rachel "A ewe lamb"—remarkable and true representations of our first two children, but not nearly so profound as the next three.

"Jordan" means "The descender" or "One who precedes". I will never forget my vision at his birth, and how he "descended" from the great hill with his paternal grandfather. In a more secular light, my Obstetrician said that without Jordan's birth preceding so closely that of the twins, it is doubtful I could have maintained a multiple pregnancy to term.

"Benjamin" means, "Son of the Right Hand" or "Favored", which, I admit without shame, he was indeed. A name of greatness in both *Old* and *New Testaments,* as well as *The Book of Mormon,* Benjamin was also my son. I smile meekly now when I think of how I worried about the difficulty he would have learning to spell and write his name in first grade.

"Matthew," as my Lord had promised, means, "Gift of God".

My own name was changed from that given me at birth. When I decided, after meeting Eric, to turn my life toward the gospel, I chose a Scandinavian version of Christine, meaning, "Follower of Christ". I went to court to have it changed legally before my marriage to Eric.

No angels came down and told me to change it; it wasn't anything like a lightning flash. It was simply that I had decided to commit myself to following my Savior, Jesus Christ, and I felt that a good Christian name would help me. I believe it has helped to keep me focused on that higher goal.

While doing our genealogy several years after our marriage, we were surprised to discover another Kirstin Rasmussen. Since she was on Eric's side of the family, we felt it must mean that we'd "chosen rightly" in marrying each other.

Soon after Ben died, a friend called to tell us she was pregnant with her sixth child, and of her experience in choosing his name.

"I was in the parking lot, getting into the car after I put in the groceries, and a voice in my mind said, *'It's a boy. His name is Joseph.'*

I asked her if it had said, *"And thou shalt call his name, Joseph".* *"No,"* she said. *"Nothing flowery like that; just, 'It's a boy, His name's Joseph'.* The funny thing is, I wasn't even thinking about it at the time. It just popped in there."

"Well," I said. "I think you'd better name him Joseph."

"But we want a girl, and we don't really like the name 'Joseph' because it usually gets shortened to 'Joe' or 'Joey'."

I laughed. I'd been through this process several times. My "Sarah" turned out to be Jordan, Matthew, *and* Benjamin. (If Jordan *had* been "Sarah", there most likely wouldn't have been a Matthew or Benjamin.)

A few months later, my friend's husband called with the good news. "It's a boy!" He exclaimed. "We've decided to call him 'Joseph'."

"Wise choice," I answered.

What struck me as funny is how attentive Joseph's father is to little Joseph. It's as if now, on his sixth child, he's finally realized how completely delightful it is to be a parent. He speaks of him incessantly, showing photos and acting like a first-time Dad.

These are the last days, and I know the Lord has saved his mightiest soldiers for the final battle against Satan. It seems that they are coming; all the little Matthew's and David's, Joseph's and Jordan's. There are, I'm sure, a few Rachel's, Sarah's, Esther's and Elizabeth's. Maybe even a Kofi Ayi, Wang Tsan, Daud Hasib Mohammed or a Pemkili Chamji Gyelzen.

I see churches of every denomination lining up on the Lord's side. We can't fight depravity alone; none of us can. We will need a united front as we enter these last days.

As we fight the war between good and evil, it is comforting to know that God has His mighty warriors in heaven as well as on earth. We will need all the help we can get from the other side. I'm gratified to know that Benjamin will be among those heavenly legions.

Rachel with Benjamin
May 3, 1991 at Good Samaritan

CHAPTER 14

One Eternal Round

A t the funeral, our friend, Sherée Fitzgerald, began Ben's service by singing "Families Can Be Together Forever." From my vantage point on the stand, I watched the spirit practically pour into the hearts of our many friends, as they began to glimpse a small piece of the possibility of a life after this one.

Sherée had been a lifeline to me many years before. I was living in Walnut Creek, working as a nanny for a family who didn't believe in God at all. Atheism was a new concept for me, and I found myself enjoying weekend outings and ski trips with them instead of going to church.

Sherée was my Visiting Teacher. She admitted to me later that she had been "afraid" when she came to invite me, an inactive sister, to a Young Adult party.

It was at that party where Eric and I met for the very first time. We spoke only briefly, but whatever was said managed to melt my fence-sitting heart. As I drove home, I began crying so hard I had to pull over to the side of the road. I prayed that I would someday be worthy of a righteous man like Eric. Once home, I blew years worth of dust from my *Book of Mormon*, and read until the light of dawn touched my rooftop window.

How I thanked my Heavenly Father for Sherée and her companion, Gaylee Beck, who overcame their fears to invite me back into activity. After that party, I put my house in order. Eric and I didn't see each other again for two more years, but I feel these two women were personally responsible for the eventual formation of our eternal family.

As I listened to Sherée sing, part of me ached for her. My eyes went from Sherée to Jill. They are outstanding women; beautiful inside and out. Each had fulfilled successful missions, had advanced college degrees and good careers. Jill, on the staff of a large university and Sherée, a recording artist, sharing the gospel through her music. Both are in their thirties, and have never married. Neither knows the joy of motherhood, nor the pain of losing a child.

Suddenly I grew warmer down to the core of my soul. Righteous women: there seemed to be so many more of them than righteous men. Benjamin, too, was righteous, and he, like so many other infant males, was dead. Only he wasn't dead. His spirit was very much alive. It was also not an infant, for when his spirit spoke to mine, it was as a man. I knew his voice. He had spoken to my mind three times. Once, as my miscarried embryo in 1980, once as an infant in my arms, and once, three days before, as I held his lifeless body at the hospital.

I cannot comprehend eternity, but I envision a strand of pearls stretching from my hand to the most distant star one can see. I picture the pearls orbiting around that star, and coming back to me again, over and over, and when I can't imagine it any more, I return to the pearl in my hand and clasp the last to the first. One eternal round; a necklace to forever—infinity.

My journey around that string of pearls will never end. My life here, the seventy or so years I may exist, is only as big as a speck of dust on but one of those uncountable trillions of pearls. Benjamin's life lasted barely four tenths of one percent of that speck of dust. Not much of a dust speck, but when compared to the multi-trillion strands of celestial pearls, does it make a difference in the overall look of his eternal necklace?

"Families can be together forever, through God's eternal plan..." Sherée sang out, her voice clear and beautiful.

Would the Lord God leave these righteous women single in the eternities? I cannot comprehend it. He has a plan, and like all his plans, it is a perfect plan. Would my Benjamin be alone forever? Never.

Marriage, like baptism, is a physical covenant, and cannot be performed in heaven. *(Mark 12:25)* Latter-day Scripture has restored many of the temporal (physical) covenants *(I Corinthians 15:29)* and these sacred ordinances are performed today in temples throughout the world. *(Doctrine and Covenants 127:6-9)* If it is necessary, Benjamin will be able to receive his covenants at a later time.

If these righteous women do not marry in this life, I know Heavenly Father has a plan for them to be sealed eternally to a man worthy of the women they have proven to be here on earth. Perhaps they are too good for any of the men on the planet at this time.

It is comforting to feel that the state of these women I love is not something about which I need worry. The Father of us all knows our needs, and will fulfill everything as it should be, in His own time. My job is to accept His will, and be happy about it. It was interesting for me to understand that Jill has already accepted His will, and is happy.

Tears never fell from my eyes as I said the opening prayer for Benjamin's funeral. I felt only love and gratitude for having Ben as long as we did, and for all the friends who came to help us through this difficult day.

Sherée sang a song from her album, *"The Spirit In All Things"* called, *"Where Is Heaven?"* I had to marvel at how that song affected me. The first time I heard it, I remember shedding tears, and thinking, quite oddly as I reflect now, what a lovely song it would be to hear at a child's funeral.

When I was asked which songs and singers I would choose for Ben's funeral, I knew. Just like the white suit he wore, there was no choice to make. It was as if I'd planned it in advance, and somehow, I think that may be true.

"Our birth is but a sleep and a forgetting:
The soul that rises with us, our life's star,
Hath had elsewhere its setting,
And cometh from afar;
Not in entire forgetfulness,
And not in utter nakedness,
But trailing clouds of glory do we come
From God, who is our home:
Heaven lies about us in our infancy!

—*William Wordsworth, poet, 1770-1850*

Not in entire forgetfulness...

Human and heavenly support sustained us this day.

Eric spoke, and I not only didn't cry, but laughed a little and shook my head when he told Matthew's "Belching Sailor" experience, thinking it had been Benjamin. It happens with twins.

Rachel got up to sing, *"I Lived In Heaven,"* and my heart raced in trepidation. I saw her look at his tiny white casket as she walked to the stand, and when she looked at me, I feared for her; I didn't know if she could sing. She had chosen the song herself, and said she wanted to sing it as her last song for Benjamin. Now she looked to me, and I wanted to rush over and hold her and tell her she didn't have to sing it; that it was all right if she wanted to change her mind.

Rachel smiled sweetly at me, and I saw the same heavenly angels surrounding her who were holding me. She nodded to the pianist, Bonnie Barberi, who played the introduction on the organ.

At the back of the room I noticed Rachel's former pediatrician slipping into a pew. Rachel saw him, too, and looked pleased.

"I lived in heaven a long time ago, it is true," she sang out, strong and sure. *"Lived there and loved there with people I know, so did you..."*

She sang without fear or hesitation, with a boldness and joy that warmed hearts throughout the building. Tears streamed down nearly every face but Rachel's, as she delivered her final gift to her baby brother.

Never have I been so proud of her, or loved her more.

Months later, when sadness would threaten to overtake me, I found solace in playing back the tape we recorded that day. Rachel's sweet voice never failed to pull me up from the shadows to the light.

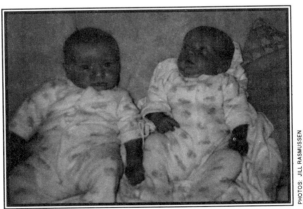

Friday, June 14, 1991. The day before he died. Was Ben looking heavenward for a reason?

CHAPTER 15

Shadows to the Light

J an Unter, Jane's husband, delivered a talk on the plan of salvation, and life after death. Quoting from the prophet Alma,

v11   "Now, concerning the state of the soul between death and the resurrection—Behold, it has been made known unto me by an angel, that the spirits of all men, as soon as they are departed from this mortal body, yea, the spirits of all men, whether they be good or evil, are taken home to that God who gave them life.

v12   And then shall it come to pass, that the spirits of those who are righteous are received into a state of happiness, which is called par-adise, a state of rest, a state of peace, where they shall rest from all their troubles and from all care, and sorrow.

v13   And then shall it come to pass, that the spirits of the wicked, yea, who are evil...these shall be cast out into outer darkness...because of their own iniquity...

v14   Thus they remain in this state, as well as the righteous in paradise, until the time of their resurrection." (Alma 40:11-14)

"Because he was pure, little Benjamin has gone to the Spirit world's Paradise to await his resurrection," Jan said.

Jan also had a story to tell about Benjamin. His son, Robert, is close in age to my son, David. Robert had spent the night at our house a few nights before, and the two had played with the babies. Robert was shaken to hear of Ben's death, and Jan held him and asked him to describe his feelings.

"Struggling to hold back big tears, Robert said to me, 'I felt like Benjamin was my own little brother.' You see, Robert is surrounded by three sisters and wishes he had a little brother. Robert fondly recalled that what he remembers most about Benjamin is that, unlike his brother Matthew, Ben would let Robert hold him without fussing. Robert said, 'Benjamin would just look gently into my eyes. It's like Benjamin really knew me.'"

At this point in his talk, my chest burned with warmth, and I thought again of Ben's eyes. Those all-seeing eyes. He probably did know Robert. I think he knew us all.

Jan continued, "Robert, Benjamin probably did know you, like many of the rest of us, from a pre-existent life we lived in before coming to this earth. And you, along with his parents, family, and friends, will yet see him again after this mortal life."

I realized that I knew absolutely that this was true. As we sang the closing hymn and Niel, Eric's brother, offered the Benediction, I felt complete peace.

As we filed out of the chapel, I saw many friends. Each of them had signed Benjamin's Baby Book. Beside Sherée's signature I glanced at her notation: *"Those who sing, pray twice."* I liked that observation.

Kimberly Pitts, Benjamin's pediatrician, was there, and I gave her a little hug.

"He was your first, wasn't he?" I asked.

"Yes," she said. "The first in my private practice."

I knew it had been difficult for her, too.

Outside, we thanked the many people who had come to offer support, many taking a whole day off work to be with us.

Old friends Jim and Carol Wooldridge were there. When Matthew was in the hospital and I needed a friend, I called Carol. Her son, Steven, took a message to call me at the hospital, and I wondered if she would even get it. A few minutes later, she was right there, standing in the hallway. She didn't even know what had happened, but she knew I needed her, and she came.

I felt ashamed of ever thinking I didn't need or have time for friends. In the clearer picture I now saw of life, they were one of the few things that really did matter.

Missionaries were busy talking to our friends and neighbors, and it seemed everyone was smiling. It was exactly as I had hoped; a celebration of Benjamin's eternal progression.

Our neighbors, Delores and Vince, were there with their children. We had been through many trials together over the years, and I was so happy to see them. Nick, the oldest boy, hugged me, and then Vince said, "God, I feel great! I've been to a lot of funerals in my life, and this isn't like any other funeral I've ever been to. I feel...happy..."

I hugged him and said, "That's the spirit you're feeling. It's telling you that the things you heard today are true."

"Yeah," Vince said, still smiling. "I feel it!"

Looking over the many faces, I saw happiness in each one. People from Hewlett-Packard, old friends, new friends from my camera club, church friends, aunts, uncles, and cousins were there.

Walking outside, I saw Benjamin's casket in the back of our new van. A rush of understanding hit me.

Our van was new, and pure, and white. It was what we needed to carry our son's body to his resting place. A big black hearse wasn't what we needed. It wasn't us. And the old "blue bomber," well, even with a new transmission, it may not have made it up the hill to the cemetery. We rode together, our family of seven, for the very last time in this earthly life. It felt right.

Many things were right...things that fit the day, and the days before...our white dresses...the bright sunshine...our friends, neighbors, and family...Sherée, singing a song I had heard year's ago, and been struck at it's appropriateness for a child's funeral, never supposing that funeral would be my own son's...my sister, Jill, visiting from 3,000 miles away, in June, instead of her usual two-day December visit; here at the crisis-point of my life, with time to stay and comfort me...Benjamin's burial suit, shown to me as if unseen hands knew I would be needing it soon...the new van...an extravagance I had hated, until I saw how perfectly Ben's little white casket fit into the back...a use Eric never suspected when he bought it for his expanding family, seven weeks before...long-forgotten memories rekindled of dreams and visions of a beautiful baby, a twin boy, who would come, but could not stay...

Eric's brother, John, drove us the hour and a half to the cemetery. On the way, we put the van's VCR to use by watching a video I had taped from a television movie. It was called, *"Go Toward The Light"* and was about a Latter-day Saint boy who died of AIDS. I had taped it a couple of years before, and remembered that it was uplifting. I hoped it could help us get through the long, sad ride. I had forgotten that the boy who died was also named Benjamin.

We all cried, but it was good for us to cry. One part showed the grandfather hand-carving a wooden box with the name, "Ben". I wondered if somehow I had subconsciously remembered that scene, which was why I had wanted a similar casket for my own little Ben.

The video finished as we came into town near the cemetery.

We stopped at a party store and got four helium-filled balloons. Rachel's was pink, David's blue, Jordan's white, and Matthew's was all three colors, swirled into a cloud. I asked the woman at the store to put two ribbon strings on it. I tried not to cry, but I thought of the other hand, the one that would never hold a balloon, and I did cry.

We drove in silence to the gravesite in Lafayette.

After Eric prayed and dedicated the grave, each child let go of his balloon, symbolic of saying good-bye. Matthew's balloon, due no doubt to the additional ribbon, did not soar heavenward with the others at first, but tarried near the ground, as if reluctant to leave.

Perhaps the answer to *"Where Is Heaven?"* was true. Sherée had sung, *"When you're with the ones you love, it's right where you are."*

We lined up behind Ben's casket for our first and last complete family portrait. We all tried to smile.

Later, Jill showed me two candid pictures taken of the twins. Both were different, yet had remarkable similarities. In the first, they were each seated in their swings. Matthew, on the left, was looking at the camera, and seemed very connected to what was going on with the photographer. Benjamin, on the right, was looking up, and seemed to be communicating with someone in the air on his right. Beside and beneath him, on the floor, was a blue ball with colored swirls in it. It looked very much like the planet earth.

In the second photograph, a close-up view of the twins on the sofa, Matthew was again on the left and connected to the photographer. Benjamin, on the right, was once again looking up and to his right; heavenward; ignoring the action taking place. Beside and beneath him was a round, blue, bulb syringe. Both photos were taken the day before Ben died.

I don't propose that the photos "mean" anything of a cosmic nature, but we were all struck by the similar compositional elements of the two photographs, and the symbolism they seemed to represent.

On the drive back to San Jose, Eric mentioned that his mother made special arrangements to have Benjamin buried beside Leland rather than in the usual children's section. I was so thankful. It was the one thing we knew Benjamin wanted. We both felt the funeral had gone exactly as Benjamin wanted it, right down to the hymn choices.

Me, Eric, Jill and the kid in front of the Oakland Temple

CHAPTER 16

Friends and Family

I t was over. I had always thought it sounded odd when newspapers printed, "survived by" (unless those mentioned had lived through a ship-wreck). Now I understood. I felt as if I had accomplished some great feat of strength. I knew nothing I would ever face would be as difficult as the past four days. The hard part was done. Life, for the rest of us, had to continue.

Our table seemed empty each meal time. Though Benjamin had never really sat there with us, there was a big, gaping hole where his place should have been. It wasn't a hole you could see, but each heart in our family felt it deeply.

Time began to be told as "two days before Ben died" or "the day after Ben died." We had to force ourselves to stop counting time.

One of my dresser drawers had unofficially become "Ben's drawer." I started putting things there...the pajamas he wore that night...his tee-shirt, cut open with scissors by the paramedics...my multicolored dress...a silver spoon, engraved with his name, but never used.

Those first few months after the funeral we survived entirely upon direction from the Lord. Even simple tasks were impossible without divine guidance.

One afternoon, when I was all alone, I heard on the radio that pediatricians were now recommending that newborn babies be placed only on their sides or backs, and never on a sheepskin due to an increased possibility of S.I.D.S.

"I knew it," I sobbed. "I could have saved him if I'd only listened to the Holy Ghost and put him up beside Matthew."

My crying grew worse and worse, and again I wanted to die myself.

Suddenly a knock came on our front door. I decided to ignore it and hide in my room, but Elder Michael Boone pushed the door open.

"Hello, Sister Youngberg," he called pleasantly, knocking again. "I just wanted to stop by to see how you're doing."

Elder Boone's mission companion was in a wheelchair, and had decided to wait in the car. I was glad. I didn't want both of them to see my tears.

I blubbered out to him what I had just heard on the radio, and my own fears.

"Before I came on my mission," Elder Boone said, "I drove an ambulance. I was a paramedic. I saw about seven cases of S.I.D.S. In five of those cases, the babies were on their backs. Nobody really knows what causes S.I.D.S., but I know one thing. I know it wasn't your fault. Benjamin was called home, and he answered his call. I just wanted you to know that."

Comfort and peace came again to my troubled soul, and I thanked Elder Boone for coming when I needed him.

"I just followed the spirit," he said. "That's my job."

Now I find myself warning new mothers to keep newborn babies on their backs or sides, and not to bundle them with too many blankets or put anything soft near their faces. Inside I know that no matter what we mortals do, precious babies will continue to do as the Lord directs.

Later, Jill reminded me of the story of Samuel the Lamanite, a prophet from *The Book of Mormon*. He went to Zarahemla to teach the Nephites about Jesus Christ, and to warn them to repent of their sins. After they cast him out, the Lord told him he had to go back and teach them again. (Helaman 13:2-4)

If Benjamin had been meant to stay with us in this life, and if turning him over would have prevented his death, the Holy Ghost would have warned me a third time.

Too many people and too many circumstances were in position for Benjamin's death not to have been part of our Lord's plan. Still, small things often upset me.

One day I saw another ambulance. It reminded me of what ambulances always remind me of now—the one that took my baby away. The one that never brought him back.

I wondered exactly when Ben died. Was it at the house? Before I picked him up, or after? Did he die in the ambulance, on the way to the hospital, or in that small white operating room?

Suddenly I remembered something that should have been so elementary. So many children have fallen into pools, or been hit by cars, or, yes, even suffocated, and they've been revived. Ben was not revived, though we found him right away. Emergency help was right there, and yet he died. Why?

Eric said that while he was asking why, an understanding came into his mind. He tried to explain it to me by likening it to a rocket that loses its booster-rocket, but then said, "No, it's easier to think of it like the starter on a car. The engine starts, and once the motor is cranked up, it goes by itself. It no longer needs the starter." I guess I still looked puzzled.

"Don't you see?" Eric asked. "Ben's body was like a car that had a good starter, but a bad engine. As long as the starter was on, his engine worked. Once the starter quit, his motor couldn't run alone." I tried hard to understand his technological explanation.

"The "engine" represents our brain or metabolism, or respiratory system, or something; I don't know," Eric continued. "Whatever the system, it won't run by itself without a preliminary "booster" or "starter" at the time we're born. Some small percentage of the bodies born in this world come without a properly functioning "engine"; missing or fouled plugs, bad fuel pump, or whatever. This is really a crude approximation, but the "starter" system masks these deficiencies for as long as it runs, which is from the time we're born (maybe before?) to between two weeks and one year."

"Science has not yet uncovered the "engine" or "engine function" which is described here, so it is called S.I.D.S." Eric continued in his brilliant engineer manner, "I guess the "starter" does such a good job of masking it that they probably haven't been (and maybe won't be) able to find it. I think Heavenly Father knew that. I think He knows that about all the S.I.D.S. babies. They come only for a short time. They can't be revived because they don't have the whole engine."

Born to die? As strange as it sounded, it made sense. It also fit my theory that I had carried Benjamin twice. He was also David's twin, but since he was born only to gain a physical body and then die, he had to have that "engine" that could shut off within the first year of his life, so he could return to fulfill his heavenly mission with the benefit of his earthly body.

When Benjamin was David's fraternal twin, his "engine" was a bit too defective. It couldn't quite last the nine months it would take to develop in my womb, and his body was miscarried.

Personally, I believe S.I.D.S. is the Lord's "on-off" switch; when he has to call them home quickly and painlessly, that is how it is accomplished.

We really felt the need to go to the Temple, but Matthew was now nursing so well, I was afraid of upsetting his schedule. It would take six hours counting the driving to attend a session in the Oakland Temple. I knew the only way to accomplish it would be to take Matthew and his heart-apnea monitor with us. Tami Kusch, our bishop's daughter, came along to watch him in the waiting room while Eric and I attended a session.

"You're not supposed to do that," the man at the recommend desk scolded when he saw Matthew. It fell to me to implore him to bend the rules. He did. We had a marvelous experience and Matthew slept until we were walking down the long hall to pick him up.

As we were healing our hearts, I remember Eric once remarking, "You know, if there ever was a 'right time' for Ben to die, then this was it. Enough time for us to know him, but not enough to have established too many good times or holidays together."

I wanted to have another baby right away. It made little sense; I knew I couldn't replace Benjamin, and I had Matthew, still a nursing baby needing my full attention.

My doctor understood. His own mother had lost a child, and until the day she died, she wanted, and could not have, another child.

After much prayer, we finally accepted our family as complete for this life. We knew that having another child could seriously jeopardize my health, and we also knew that if Matthew couldn't fill the void left by Benjamin, nobody else could either. We left open the possibility of adoption later.

One day I read that a foster family was needed for five Hispanic sisters who didn't want to be separated. My heart ached for them, and when I read the article to Eric, he said, "If I had the room, they'd be here."

His answer made my heart feel glad again.

Eric returned to work after only a week's absence. I didn't want him to go, and was a bit of a baby myself, but I realized how much he needed to get on with his life, which included his work as well as our family.

Rachel had auditioned for the play *Heidi* the day we picked Jill up from the airport. We found out she got the part of *Clara* the day Benjamin died.

She had also committed to sing a solo for our 6th Ward Reunion, to be held only a week after Ben died.

Rachel went on performing, including *Heidi,* and seemed to add even greater depth to her characters as she showed real tears on stage with a mere thought of Benjamin. Her nightly portrayals of Belinda Cratchet in *A Christmas Carol* even made the director cry. Driving her to the frequent rehearsals, fittings, and performances was tedious, but good for me.

We knew we needed time to heal, but we also felt that keeping busy schedules might help us to get past the pain more easily. As ridiculous as it may sound, we also felt Benjamin would want us to move forward.

We put off our plan to sell the house. It hurt every time I entered the nursery. I wanted desperately to sell everything and start over. Our living room table was no longer the place for picture books, but where Benjamin lay as Jill had administered CPR. Every turn reminded me of something sad.

Later, David was upset and he finally exploded in tears at having to use Ben's dresser. We had been in the middle of changing dressers, and stenciling little toy trains on them when Ben died. I had completely forgotten David was using the dresser with Benjamin's name stenciled on it.

Jordan and Matthew occupied most of my time. Matthew's monitor was cumbersome and noisy, but I got used to it. Once it went off for a low heart rate, and it frightened me, but the Holy Ghost was right beside me, reminding me Matthew has a long life ahead.

For the first few months, I seemed to need to tell everyone about Benjamin. Mostly I talked to sales clerks. One poor photo dealer asked me about the twins when I looked at their photos.

"Isn't he precious?" I said. "He died."

A woman in the mall stopped to tell me how cute Matthew was, and I said, "So was his twin brother, but he died."

I felt awful, saying things like that, but I couldn't seem to stop it. I felt I was somehow betraying Benjamin if I allowed someone to coo over Matthew without knowing about his twin brother. Time seems to have stopped most of my confessions.

One time I did feel I should mention my twin who died, and it happened that the woman with whom I spoke had also lost a twin. It was odd, because she needed to talk about it, and I met her in a grocery store several miles from my home. I had never shopped there before, and wondered why I had decided to stop there instead of my usual store. I do feel I was directed to meet her that night.

Sometimes my words seemed inspired, like the time I was crying in a rest room after seeing my first opera. It was about a nun who had a child who died. Another woman was there in the rest room with me, trying to be brave. She was an older woman, and had lost her only child many years before. She chastised herself for being upset, as he had lived only three hours. I held her and rubbed her back, and she cried and cried and cried for the precious son she had never even been allowed to hold.

I shared with her my testimony, and we have become friends.

It is difficult when people ask us how many children we have, and it probably always will be hard to discuss. Eric listened to me many nights as I cried about these things. One night he said, "When people ask me how many children I have, I'm saying 'five'. We do have five children. One of them is just not here with us right now."

Daredevil Matthew on his roller blades at 14 months. June, 1992

CHAPTER 17

Following the Spirit

Whenever I thought about Christmas, I cried. I knew I couldn't unwrap that "pea pod" ornament. I knew I couldn't take the manger scene out of the box. I couldn't put only six stockings on the mantle.

It made me so angry! There had been a family in one of our wards who had lost a daughter. I remembered going to their home at Christmas time and seeing a sock with her name on it, though she had been dead for six years. I remembered thinking how maudlin that seemed. How I thought I'd never do that if I ever lost a child. Now I understood.

Probably the most difficult thing for me was not having a family photograph. We had taken four pictures at the hospital, but two were out of focus, and the other two had the twins' faces covered in their isolettes. This would be the only Christmas I could send a photograph of the entire family, and I busied myself enlarging and reducing, cutting and pasting different photographs together until

I had a poor but passable representation.

Now I understood why the family portrait I had always envisioned was not a photograph, but a painting. In it, I am seated in the center, holding Jordan, and Eric is standing behind me. David and Rachel are standing beside him, and they each hold our babies. One day I will meet the artist who can paint us together, and we will have our family portrait.

Understanding has come with age, and I suppose that is why wisdom is rarely found in the young. It takes a long time to walk in each person's moccasins.

One day, shortly after Benjamin died, I was distracted by thoughts of him, and made a minor mistake in traffic. Angry commuters raced around me, yelling profanities, and I burst into tears. Later, a pedestrian ran in front of me, against the light. Instead of my usual nasty Type-A, hyper reaction, I found myself thinking, *"I hope he's all right"* and I whispered a prayer for his well-being. I realized that I loved that stranger. He was my brother. I truly cared about him and his trials through this life.

Many years ago I recall feeling appalled at the messiness of a young mother's house. *"Why doesn't she put those clothes away, or wipe off that countertop?"* I'd thought. Now I know the utter impossibility of 'doing it all' in a home full of toddlers, when sheer exhaustion prevents clean sheets every week, or dinner on time. When two tiny children manage to empty a fifty pound bag of potting soil onto the living room carpet and drive their trucks through it before you finish making one bed upstairs.

You only had it in the house to start your garden, and two days later the same two children do the same thing in the same place with your year's supply of powdered sugar. Oh, I know. It was Jordy and Maffy, and my living room, stairs, front hall, and half of the dining room. I'm still finding bits of it in the carpet.

I hope I live long enough to be able to visit the homes of young mothers, fold their clothes, and wash their toddler's faces. Young mothers always need help; someone who has been there to offer comfort and support.

These subtle changes in my attitude have come about recently, but I don't know that they are a direct result of losing my child. People have said and done many things in an effort to comfort me over my loss. Many are afraid to speak, for fear of offending me. Only one comment has made me angry, and I have heard it from many people in the church. I hope never to hear it again:

"Don't you feel your baby's death has made you a stronger and better person, and made your family closer?"

Our family has always been close. I have always been strong, too strong at times, and I hope and pray it doesn't take a death to improve someone.

Through all of this, I recognize that grieving is a lifelong process. As advice to others, I want to say that you will never forget your child. While you may feel peace in our knowledge of the life after this one, you will always miss him. He is gone for this life, and your family will never again feel or be complete.

Call on your Visiting and Home Teachers and tell them your needs. Be specific. "I really need you with me Tuesday morning. It's the anniversary of my son's death, and I don't want to be alone." We have not been commanded to "mourn with those who mourn" merely because it looked good written as scripture.

Do what you need to do in your own time. When Aunt Mindy suggests, "Isn't it time you put away his toys, dear?" Tell her you are grateful for her concern, and she can be assured you will do it as soon as you are ready.

To the friends of those grieving: Don't decide to cure someone of their sorrow by removing all memories of the departed one. A woman told me her Relief Society sisters had cleared out her baby's entire nursery and turned it into a guest room before she returned from the hospital. She missed an important grieving step, and has never fully recovered.

Many Latter-day Saints seem to feel families who lose children have been somehow "blessed" to have a "valiant spirit"; a child already in the Celestial Kingdom. Some look at me in awe, and reverently ask how I felt, being "chosen" as the mother of one so great.

Buzz. Reality check needed.

While we have often felt blessings and the peace and comfort of the Holy Ghost, our family is not better than another family because we lost a child. We were not "chosen" because we are somehow more righteous than another family. We're not, and we haven't handled it any better or worse than any other family would, given similar circumstances. The death of a child is not a blessing we hope others "get to" experience.

Don't fear or reject antidepressant drugs. If it weren't for my daily dose, I'd still be sitting in my rocking chair, wet with tears, clutching the jammies he wore when he died. Medicine has come a long way; if you need it, follow your physician's advice. Eric and the older children know when I have skipped a dose. "Did you forget to take your medicine?" has become a familiar question in our home. I am appalled that 98% of the time, they are right. Those who can benefit from love, care, and Priesthood Blessings receive my heartiest congratulations. Others, like me, can only be chemically balanced with competent psychiatric care and regular, perhaps even lifelong, drug therapy.

Serve others who have lost children. You have been there, and your understanding love is often the thing they need most. Nobody understands more than someone who has lived through the same experience. I remember snapping at one social worker who came to help me while Matthew was hospitalized. She put her arms around me and said she understood. "Have you ever lost a child?" I demanded. When she said she had not, I asked her to leave. In those first days, I could only accept help from those who had felt my pain in their own lives. I knew I could trust them and believe what they said to me. The others, I felt, were "hired help."

Eric knew it would be difficult, if not impossible, for me to go through that first Christmas season after Ben's death. We had always stayed at home, and over the years had created many family traditions. David and Rachel wanted to continue as before, but on this one point I was firm in my own needs.

"Next year, we will continue our traditions," I said. "but this year, we're on the road."

It was the best decision I made. We packed all the kids, bottles, diapers, and playthings into the new van. We threw in some presents, video games and tapes, gassed up, and were on our way.

We took the first leg of the trip to Phoenix with the Unter's beside us in their van. Jane's parents took us in overnight. It was wonderful to meet them and see where Jane's loving heart was nurtured.

We visited the Grand Canyon, Carlsbad Caverns, and even spent a day shopping in Mexico. We ended up in Temple, Texas, where we stayed with Eric's brother Niel, and their children. We felt Terry, our sister-in-law, deserved a medal. She had driven by herself from Temple to San Jose in a double-cab pick-up truck with all five children, nearly three days straight through, to be on time for Benjamin's funeral.

Spending Christmas with them was exactly what we needed. Having a big family around us...noisy—messy—kids everywhere... was wonderful. My favorite part was driving around Temple's beautifully lighted and decorated neighborhoods with all the kids in the back of the truck, singing Christmas Carols as loudly as possible to Kurt Bestor's Airus Christmas music tape, which Niel blared out of the gigantic speakers in his truck.

Always, we'll be thankful to the family who lives in "the middle of nowhere" Texas, who had their Christmas lights lit at two o'clock in the morning. We were exhausted from hours of driving, with hours to go, when we came upon the lights. They featured a hand-cut-and-painted set of Santa Claus in his sleigh, being pulled by eight tiny *armadillos!*

Our children have grown and flourished this past year. David seems to have an understanding of Ben's death of which I am at times envious. When I am down, he brings me up, and likewise I help him. So far we have managed not to be sad at the same time. David is involved in many programs at school and we know we have a future scientist in our midst. Like his father, David also plays the saxophone.

Rachel's talents have blossomed, and she has recorded her first song, *"A Silver Bracelet"*, and a music video. Her strength is in spiritual songs, which she performs in churches of all denominations. She hopes to eventually study opera. It is a challenge having a future opera singer in my home. (I confess I do not yet fully appreciate this type of music, but I understand I, too, have many years to learn.) Her goal for next year is to perform a solo with the Mormon Tabernacle Choir.

Rachel is always looking for cloud's silver linings. One day as she read the funny papers, she happened on a comic from "The Family Circus" by Bil Keane. "Since Ben died," Rachel said, "our family is just like theirs; David is Billy, I'm Dolly, Jordy is Jeffy, and Maffy is P.J.—When can we get a dog like Barfy?" Kids. They never seem to quit trying.

She is right about Bil Keane's "family". His comic often features "guardian angels," of which our family has many.

Jordan is calm, silly, and he loves music. He remembers Benjamin and will sometimes get out our photo albums and talk about him. Matthew is another story.

So many times I have been thankful for Eric's vision of Matthew's future mission, if for no other reason than to assure myself that he will survive to be at least nineteen. This child has several full-time guardian angels. Jordy plays hard, but is seldom ever injured. Matthew is wild. As I wrote this paragraph, he and Jordy climbed on our exercise bicycle. Jordy jumped off, unscathed. Matthew, just fifteen months old, fell and broke his arm.

Matthew thinks that when a door in our home opens, it is his job to wiggle through it and run to the center of the street. He stands there, grinning, as if he expects to be awarded a medal for successfully escaping to his target. From the time he took his first step-at eight months like his two older siblings—(David was the only normal child, walking on his first birthday), Matthew has been one solid bruise. He climbed over or under, or through every baby gate we tried for the sheer pleasure of cart-wheeling down the stairs. He's burned his hand on our lawnmower (I was cautious when it was on and didn't fathom danger once it was off.) He had stitches in his forehead. At the baby pool, he fell in, and my friend Loretta claims she didn't know I could move so fast. His guardian angels got there first. By the time I scooped him up, he yelled a steady stream of heated baby-curses at me; he was angry, but miraculously had held his breath and floated until I got him.

Sometimes I think God took Benjamin back because he knew I would need half the hosts of heaven just to chase Matthew. Benjamin seems to have given Matthew all of his earthly spunkiness—a double-dose! I picture Benjamin up there on the other side, cheering Matthew along to make me run faster.

At other times I worry that God took him back because He knew I couldn't handle him, or wouldn't do a good job raising him. When I feel that way, I fear I let my husband and family down. Usually I cry and then I say a prayer, and I know that all is well.

If I allow myself to fear, and doubt God's plan, I find myself rapidly spinning into a whirlpool of despair. My tears can fall for hours at a time. When at last I stop from sheer exhaustion, I realize no release. Tears bring no relief from the pain-they only extend it. Like recalling long-forgiven sin, dwelling on painful memories serves Lucifer; not my Heavenly Father.

Often I have sought answers to the puzzles of my life. I could drag my brain into permanent analysis over any single question. Now I am content to place nearly everything into the section labeled, "Heavenly Father's Plan".

When I have trouble believing this, I drag out a tattered letter. It is neatly printed on plain "college ruled" white notebook paper by a fourteen year old girl I had never met. Her name is Lisa Dominici, and she lives in New York State.

Lisa is LDS, and, according to Jill, she is a "very good and exceptionally spiritual" student in my sister's seminary class.

A few months after Ben's death, Jill sent me this letter from Lisa.

"Usually my dreams are pretty outrageous and ridiculous. But this one particular night about two weeks before Jill left to go back home, I had this one dream that seemed so lifelike and incredibly real.

I dreamt that Jill went to her sister's house and was able to visit with the family and play with her twin nephews for a couple of days. Then around the third morning or so, Jill went into the boys room to get them up and one of the babies had died. My dream continued on to show the grieving and deep sorrow the family felt but then it suddenly stopped and I woke up.

I continued to think about it throughout the next couple of weeks. I think because it seemed so realistic to me. But there was no way possible I was going to tell Jill about it.

Close to two weeks later, while Jill was out west, I had the same dream again, only this time it was shorter. It started when Jill walked into the twin's room and ended at the same time.

The Sunday Jill came back to church, it was fast and testimony meeting. As soon as Jill walked up to the podium I knew what she was going to say."

Lisa Dominici, 1991

In one of my own journals, I recorded the following dream on Thursday, March 28, 1974: *"...Suddenly I was whisked away to a futuristic place where I was viewing my house from above... A thousand questions were directed at me, and if I didn't or couldn't answer, a sharp, pricking noise would pierce my head, and I would scream in pain and frustration. They asked about my children, six of them, two sets of twins, but there were only five now, as one of the twins had died earlier..."*

This dream was so vivid, I can still recall it in detail, and feel amazed at it's accuracy. In 1974 we didn't even know we had any twins in our family, and how could I possibly know, even on a sub-conscious level, that I would one day conceive two sets of twins, let alone know that one would die?

Still, I often have a hard time accepting dreams, visions, and feelings I have as being real, personal messages to help me through this life.

It is one thing to doubt my own spiritual experiences, but when Lisa, a complete stranger living three thousand miles away confirms the Lord's will and plan, it is impossible to deny.

*At home—Rachel, 15, David, 17,
Matthew, 6 and Jordy, 8. April, 1998*

E P I L O G U E

N early seven years have passed since Benjamin died. That first summer, Eric and I took advantage of an airline price war and purchased round-trip tickets to Syracuse, New York. My mother cared for our children.

We stayed with Jill, who was then an Assistant to the Dean of Students at S.U.N.Y. in Oswego. She's grown her hair long again, and is looking lovely. Last year she started a new job at the American University in Bulgaria. She helps her neighbors and the missionaries there when she isn't working.

The highlight of our New York visit, which included trips to Canada and historic sites of the church, was attending the Hill Cumorah Pageant. We met the entire Dominici Family, who were performing in the pageant, which reenacts the coming forth of *The Book of Mormon*. When I was introduced to Lisa, I tried not to cry, but I couldn't seem to stop myself. She was, as Jill had said, a very spiritual young woman.

It took a long time, but my neighbor in San Jose, Dolores, and her daughter, took the missionary discussions. I feel it was due in part to Ben, and that in some small way, he was their first missionary. Even if they don't join our church, I feel certain the knowledge they gain will help them desire to learn more about the Savior, and live in joy, as He taught.

Nina Duarte was baptized into the church. Nina had played "Mrs. Cratchit" when Rachel was "Belinda Cratchit" in *"A Christmas Carol."* Rachel felt Nina's spirit, and suggested we give her a *"Book of Mormon."* We wrote our testimonies in the book, and included a family photo. It took nearly five years, but at her baptism, Nina said, "I guess I was one of those *"Book of Mormon"* success stories."

We have moved from our native California and settled in a lovely rural community along the Wasatch Front. I feel a peace here, and seem to gather strength from the mountains. I don't miss the pace of city life, stray bullets, or police helicopters shining lights in my backyard at three o'clock in the morning. Though I long for old friends, I am quite content to stay here forever and have them visit me. Even the local cemetery seems like a good place for my eventual rest.

Eric is my strongest support. He is never too manly to spill his tears with mine when we feel that need. We laugh more than we cry. Though his partnership fell through, and he has been virtually unemployed for three years, the time off has allowed him to work on his inventions. One now has a patent-pending, and we have high hopes for its eventual manufacture. It's called TimeSentry.™ It's a new technology that allows digital clocks on appliances, in cars and on watches to set themselves. After a power outage, clocks with his chip acquire the correct time within eight seconds, and will always be accurate to within one second. No more "Flashing 12:00" on your VCR or breadmaker! Now if we could just get G.E. or another appliance manufacturer to look at the working prototype. His technology will partially solve the year 2000 'Millennial Bug' problem.

Eric has thoroughly enjoyed being home to see the children

grow. We have been able to put our "year's supply" to the test, and so far, except for one bad week, we've been self-reliant. (Which really means The Lord provides instead of your family, the church, or government.) When things have really been tough, mysterious envelopes containing cash have appeared. We know we have been continually blessed.

David speaks to me privately about his feelings toward Ben's death, though not often. He enjoys his old and new friends, reading Sci-Fi, playing his saxophone, and designing computer web-pages. He has finished his Eagle project, and is growing (over six feet tall at age seventeen) to be a fine young man, and a credit to his name. He heads for college this year.

Rachel feels emotion deeply, and cries when she needs to cry. She is a bit big for my lap now, but we manage to cuddle into our big rocking chair, and work life out with the limited knowledge we've been given. She likes boys only from a distance, and while I know that will change, I'm still enjoying my only daughter. Rachel has expanded her singing, and using her voice brings her immense joy. She now plays cello, and is fulfilling her promised blessing of a life filled with music. Her songs bring pleasure to all who hear them, with the possible exception of her big brother. She studies opera and cello, singing an adult part in Don Giovanni with Utah Opera, and touring with the chamber orchestra. Her acting career has also blossomed, with large roles in plays (Eliza Doolittle in "My Fair Lady") and small roles in film and television shows (Fox TV, ABC TV, Universal Pictures). She is now a member of the Screen Actors Guild. Until the last week in December, when Hewlett-Packard paid Eric for some consulting work he had done, Rachel had made more money that year than Eric and I combined. She loves being able to give us loans and surprise us with something we thought we couldn't afford. She bought our Christmas tree one year. Rachel is fifteen, and is always willing to serve. She sings whenever she is asked (baptisms, Nursing Homes, and community events) and volunteers at the local library, teaching reading and acting out stories for the children. She wants to study classical opera at Juilliard.

Jordan is eight and can ride a bicycle faster than I can tolerate watching. I insist they all wear helmets when they ride, so David's bike is gathering dust. Helmets are not cool here. Jordan, however, loves his helmet. I do make him take it off for bed, bath, and church. Jordy tends to boss Matthew around, but they enjoy most things together. Jordan likes third grade and learning all he can about everything. He's terrific in math.

We finally got a dog. His name is Gus, and he does resemble the mutt, "Barfy," of "Family Circus" fame. I love him as much as the kids do, and he has become a member of the family. I honestly don't know how I survived forty years without a dog.

Matthew is now almost seven and I'll fill you in on where we started in the first chapter.

A few months before his fourth birthday, Matthew had surgery to stop his sleep apnea. The operation was performed by Dr. B. Kelly Ence as outpatient surgery at Mountain View Hospital in Payson, Utah, on January 30, 1995. Three months later, he felt the need to share a sacred experience.

"I need to tell you about my surgery," Matthew said.

Tucking his blankets around him and repositioning his toys, I mumbled absently, "Sure, honey."

"I need to tell you about when I died," he whispered.

"You didn't die," I blurted immediately, bumping my head on Jordy's top bunk. I fearfully recalled Dr. Ence's words about "some complications."

"Yes, I died," he insisted. "And I need to tell you what happened."

I was trying to remain calm and not react while getting the rest of the family close enough to hear what he was telling me.

If this had been Rachel, I could have laughed, and listened to her "story." Rachel was born in fantasyland, and has never grown out of it. Matthew, however, is very firmly grounded. He's never even liked fairy tales, and games of pretend are quite foreign to him. PBS nature films are about as wild as he gets.

"I saw Benjamin, Jesus Christ, and Zacharias," he stated as matter-of-factly as if he'd announced that the sun was shining.

"Zacharias!" I shrieked. "How do you know Zacharias!"

I was reeling. This kid is three years old. He's still lisping, for crying out loud! (He pronounced the name, "Thak-a-wy-uth")

We'd taught him a few very basic Bible stories. Moses in the river. Noah and the ark. Baby Jesus. He'd always said, "Jesus," not the formal "Jesus Christ," and I knew absolutely he'd never even heard the name "Zacharias." I was really not prepared for his answer.

"Oh, mom," he said, looking at me as if I was the most stupid person on earth. "When you die, you know everything."

"Jesus Christ said, 'Matthew I love you very much, but you can't stay.'" Matthew continued. "Ben said, 'It's not your time yet,' and I had to go back."

Still in shock, I asked him what Zacharias had said.

"Zacharias just stood there; he didn't say anything."

By this time, Rachel was leaning across his bed. "Did you see Heavenly Father?" she asked.

"Yes," he said. "But He was across the river with Elijah, and I couldn't go there."

Elijah. That's hardly a name we bandy about in everyday conversation. I couldn't believe this was coming from Matthew. I knew he couldn't be making this up. He didn't know enough to make it up.

By now the whole family was closing in on him, asking questions.

He didn't volunteer anything after that, and when I tried to get him to repeat what he had told me while I videotaped him the next day, he refused.

Later in the week, I asked him why he wouldn't talk about it.

"I don't like to talk about it," he said. "It makes me sad."

"Sad?" I asked. "Why does it make you sad?"

"Because I had to come back," he said simply.

Once I was relating his experience to a friend as he wandered in and out of the room. I told her he had seen Zachariah.

"No! Not Zachariah!" He complained, obviously irritated by my ignorance. "Zacharias!"

It was hard not to laugh, as that last "s" came out as a sloppy and slobbery "th."

For several days he clammed up entirely, then, during a Family Home Evening lesson, he opened up a little more.

"Everything is white," he explained. "There's a ceiling and a floor, but no walls."

When we called it "heaven," he corrected us.

"It wasn't heaven," he said. "I think it was like a 'waiting room.' It was Ben's waiting room."

He pointed to Jordan's face. "Your face doesn't look like this there," he said. "It looks like this," he explained, pointing to my bright white cotton blouse.

"Everything and everybody is bright and shiny white," he exclaimed. Except Jesus Christ has a red..." his voice trailed off and he squinted his eyes as if trying to see something. "...a red sweater?... no...coat?...no..." Then his face lit up into a big grin. "Jesus Christ has white clothes and a red blankie (blanket) on his shoulders like a coat."

David was immediately reminded of a painting of Christ often used in church. He ran to get it, and showed it to Matthew.

"That's not Jesus Christ," he complained, shaking his head, "He looks better than that."

We all thought that was funny, and David asked, "Well, what does He look like, bub?"

Matthew said, "He's all white. His face is white. His hair is white. He has short hair, like Mommy's, (I had recently had my hair cut into a short "page-boy" style) and he doesn't have a beard or a...that!" he said, pointing to His mustache. (A word not then in his vocabulary.)

We showed Matthew several pictures of Jesus, but he shook his head at every one of them.

He said Benjamin was, "taller than Daddy," and Jesus was "about as tall as Daddy." (Eric is a smidge over 6' 1" tall.) He claimed Zacharias was "short."

He said Zacharias had "long, bended (curly) hair," but when we asked about Ben's hair, Matthew seemed perplexed until I took him to the mirror and asked if it looked like his hair. Matthew's face lit up like a June bug in July, and, smiling broadly, proclaimed, "Ye'th's! Hi'th's hair i'th's yust yite mine hair!" I smiled too, to learn that his beautiful reddish-blond hair had crossed the veil with him.

Some days Matthew shares things from the other side.

"You'd like the gate," he said one day for no apparent reason.

"What gate?" I asked absently, forgetting momentarily that this child is not like other mortals.

"You know," he said, pointing heavenward. "Up there. It's all gold. It's a big gate. You'd like it."

One day, Rachel was flipping through her photo album. "Turn back the page!" he ordered. "I want to see the angel!"

Rachel turned back the page to a photograph of herself, standing with my mother and me. The camera was shooting directly into the sun, creating a back-lit corona effect around the image of my very blonde mother.

"Oh, never mind," he said sadly. "It's not an angel; it yust yoots yite one." (Just looks like one)

Matthew is the first patient Dr. Ence has had undergo an NDE, or Near-Death Experience; the medical term for Matthew's short hop behind the veil and back.

"You won't have to worry about brain damage or anything," Dr. Ence explained, perhaps concerned about a lawsuit.

I assured him I had no intention of suing, and was only curious. He then explained more fully what had happened during the surgery.

Matthew had a monitor hooked to his finger to measure the amount of oxygen in his blood. The anesthesiologist administered the drugs to put him under general anesthesia, and Matthew's reading quickly dropped. In medical terms, he "de-saturated rapidly," which means the oxygen was too low, causing his heart to stop. He explained that this can happen very fast, particularly in children.

The emergency team reacted immediately, and Matthew's heart was started "at once."

I asked Dr. Ence to define "at once."

"At the most," he replied, "Matthew's heart stopped for only one and a half to two minutes."

Startled at that obvious admission of my son's actual, recorded, clinical death, I wondered how long, approximately, two minutes would be in eternity. I was envious. I've suffered through 22 surgeries, and never had a near-death experience. Of course, I've never died, either. Maybe I don't want to experience that after all. They may not bring me back.

As I watch Matthew stomping through the snowdrifts outside, I know how very remarkable he is to me now, and marvel at what he will become as he grows. That bundle of unbridled energy, crowned with his reddish-blond halo, has seen more than I will until I join his brother in death.

I wonder still how much Benjamin was able to share with him. After all, they are twins.

He must have seen much more than he's willing to discuss, because he comes up with some intensely bizarre stuff.

One day, Matthew asked, "Is heaven up in space?"

I answered that nobody really knows its actual location.

"I do," he said. "It must be in space, because there are so many big stars and planets there. I got to see them up close."

That was it. That's all he said, and pushing for more facts gets me absolutely nowhere. I must be content to wait for him to decide when he wants to share something.

He has told us when a particular extended-family member will die, and it seems plausible. We have chosen not to share this information with the family member, though Matthew explained that it would "be (his/her) time to go." My journal is filling up with his predictions. Perhaps I'd better start his own journal.

Friends have speculated that Zacharias appeared to Matthew because he is his Guardian Angel. I wouldn't be a bit surprised. Eric and I always said Matthew had half the hosts of heaven guarding him; if not, the father of John the Baptist would be a logical choice. I mean, John was a somewhat of a wild character himself; eating locusts and honey while he hid out in the hills. Zacharias must have had his hands full, trying to train John up in the ways of the Lord. Chasing Matthew around the earth might make Zacharias feel a touch of being a mortal father again.

Knowing Matthew has a mission to look forward to on earth assures me that Benjamin, Jesus Christ, and Zacharias will continue to bless him, if only through his memory of their meeting.

Matthew knows Jesus Christ lives and loves him. He told him face to face. What inexpressible joy this gift has given our whole family.

When I think that none of this would have happened without Rachel's finger getting smashed in the gymnasium door, and reading that article, and scheduling surgery when we did...

"And we know that all things work together for good to them that love God, to them who are called according to His purpose." Romans 8:28

Rachel's finger has healed completely. Her leg is now in a cast, but her fingernail grew back, and looks as lovely as her other nine digits.

We have revisited our old ward in San Jose, and have been pleasantly surprised at its open and friendly atmosphere. We noticed many new faces, of many different colors, all seated together, sharing hymnbooks as they sing the songs of Zion.

"It all started after Benjamin's funeral," a friend confided. "Everyone seemed to realize that any of us could die suddenly, and everyone started to talk to everyone else. We've had service projects for nearly every family in the ward. Everyone gets a better garden when we plant it together. We actually had nine convert baptisms last month."

Since Matthew's experience, I no longer feel guilty for Benjamin's death. All nightmares have ceased. I feel a deep and lasting serenity. I know I, like Matthew, will see him again. I know Benjamin, like Jesus, lives. It is in a place much different from here, but I'm in no rush. I am so thankful the Lord gave me twin boys, knowing He would have to call one of them home to Him so soon.

My children are my joy. Eric and I count each day a miracle. We have our ups and downs, but the downs now seem much less important.

Someone once said that when a person dies, his loved ones lose the past, but when a baby dies, they lose the future. It is a comfort to me to know that our future does not end in this temporal lifetime. We have an eternal future together. Even so, I know I will always cry at Christmas and on Mother's Day, and though I will never let him see, I will always cry on Matthew's birthday.

I know absolutely that Benjamin was a choice spirit; a blessed and precious child of our Heavenly Father. A few times, when my faith is full, I have been able to pray my thanks to Him for taking Ben before he had to endure the trials of life. God's decision to allow Benjamin to stay in our home for six and a half weeks rather than taking him at the moment of birth, fills me with immeasurable gratitude. We were privileged to have him live with our family, no matter how short.

Matthew. My joy. My baby boy. His hair, sprouted at last, is a golden-red tone, and I now know his twin brother shares the same shade. Grandma is delighted to have another redhead in the family. It is somehow comforting to know that their hair is the same color. Though Matthew's is quite long and wispy, with curls in the back, I can't yet bear to cut it too short, and find myself touching it often. At those times, I wonder if Matthew will ever notice or even care, that when I kiss his sweet red head, I always kiss him twice.

It gives me enormous peace to know Matthew saw and spoke with his brother, and didn't find it the least bit curious that he was alive and fully grown.

... *"you will be blessed..."* the messenger had whispered.
Matthew, as his name proclaims, was my gift from God. He was, and is, the promised twin.

Benjamin, my darling babe, was never mine to keep. He was my gift to God, but he is not forever lost. I know I will see him again, on our never-ending journey through eternity.

THE END